Keys to AUTHORITY for Every Believer

BOOT CAMP

LYNN HARDY

COPYRIGHT

Lynn Hardy © 2018, 2019

The names of certain individuals mentioned in this book have been changed to protect
their privacy and identity. The events recorded herein are accurate, and have been
represented as they occurred to the best of the author's recollection and ability.

Resilient Publishing
P.O. Box 234
Star, ID 83669

ResilientPublishing.com

Keys to Authority for Every Believer
By Lynn Hardy

ISBN 9781979663342
Second Edition 2019

Table of Contents

Believers' Boot Camp Series

People think of boot camp as a place you train for combat. Any veteran will tell you that basic training is about three things:

➢ Knowing what weapons are available
➢ Learning how to use those weapons
➢ Receiving orders and following them

Believer's Boot Camp series, published in 2016–2017, is a collection of books I authored, which teaches us how to hear more clearly from God with the goal to ready ourselves for a face-to-face meeting with our Lord, Jesus. The series reveals the "weapons and tools" God has given us and how to use them, so we can bring God's kingdom to Earth. Each book in the series focuses on a single topic to clearly define one tool or weapon from our Heavenly Father.

The series uses the Word of God to reveal all that He has given us through Jesus. The Bible is our instruction manual and the Holy Spirit is our guide to understanding it. "Keys to Authority For Every Believer" clearly defines the boundaries of our authority so that the Word of

God can increase our faith as we learn how to use it.

May God flood the eyes of your heart with understanding so that you can know and understand all that He intends for you.

Books in the *Believers' Boot Camp* series:

Volume One
WHY DOESN'T GOD SPEAK TO ME?

Volume Two
KEYS TO AUTHORITY FOR EVERY BELIEVER

Volume Three
DESTROYING CURSES IN THE COURTS OF HEAVEN

Volume Four
ROADMAP TO HEAVEN

Why You Need Authority

The finest trick of the devil is to persuade you that he does not exist.

~ Charles Baudelaire

There are a number of sequels and spinoffs that were spawned by the original 1933 movie *The Invisible Man,* as well as more than one comic book hero whose coveted power of invisibility is used to their advantage. When people believe that Satan isn't involved in the things of this Earth it gives him a tremendous tactical advantage. Equally as damaging is the idea that God is not interested or active in the activities of this world. The Bible is very clear: there are two kingdoms on Earth and they are at war.

> For He has rescued us from the Kingdom of Darkness and transferred us into the Kingdom of His dear Son… (Colossians 1:13 NLT)

If you are a Christian, you are at war whether or not you know it. You have been under siege and potentially losing ground unless you are enforcing your rights. How can you win a battle if you don't know what weapons you have been given?

Authority is the most powerful weapon at our disposal. A police officer directing traffic at an intersection where electricity has failed does not stop a massive truck by the strength of his arm. The vehicle would smash him flat if he tried. The reason an officer can direct vehicles with ease in these circumstances is because of the authority they have been granted by the government that's only reinforced by our respect for that authority.

Drivers see the person in uniform, a symbol of their authority, and know that they need to obey their commands. In an emergency situation I have seen a plain clothes, off-duty officer step up to direct traffic as well. Even without the uniform, his movements are so assured and assertive that drivers still obey his commands.

Officers are stationed at busy intersections to avoid accidents and help move vehicles along smoothly. Because Christians have not been in uniform (aware of their authority), progress for the Kingdom of God has been slow and hampered. For this reason, we have lost some wonderful people, generals in the army of God, when collisions from the resulting chaos have ensued. The Bible speaks of this:

> My people are destroyed for lack of knowledge [of My law, where I reveal My will]. (Hosea 4:6)

Note to readers pertaining to passages quoted from the Amplified Bible:

• Regarding quoted scripture, bracketed words and phrases further explain the meaning of original text.

• Parentheses and dashes (–) signify additional meanings of words contained in the original text.

We must know more about God and the system He created. If we don't know what authority has been given to us, how can we use it? It is equally important to know how incredibly useful it can be. The answers are found within the Word of God.

> All Scripture is inspired by God and profitable for teaching, for reproof, for correction, for training in righteousness, so that the man of God may be adequate, equipped for every good work. (2 Timothy 3:16-17 NASB)

By learning what the inspired Word of God says, we are equipped to do our job. We cannot do our job properly if we are hindered by an enemy who we do not even realize is fighting against us. There are keys to authority God gave to man. Possessing these keys will unlock doors to health, peace, and financial provision. The goal of this book is to unlock the bonds that have kept God's people from all that He has for them by teaching the basics of authority.

My aim is to keep each book tightly focused on a single topic. If you are unsure of why God limits His interaction on this Earth or how the Bible has been scientifically proven to be the absolute true, inspired Word of God, this is discussed in the FREE book "Why Doesn't God Speak to Me?" I would recommend that you read it first.

DEFINING AUTHORITY

Before we can find the keys to our authority we must know how and when the Bible discusses the subject. The Word of God describes two separate spiritual forces that can affect this world: power and authority. Together these words are used 219 times in the New

Testament alone. Unfortunately, sometimes the Greek word for authority is translated as power. This creates some confusion about the use and application of authority.

There is a distinction in the Bible about the application of these two forces. This can be seen in the original language of this ancient text. The Greek words for power and authority are:

Dynamis (dü'-nä-mēs): The root of the words for dynamite or dynamic. It means a force in power, strength, and a mighty work. In some cases, it also translates as "miracle," "works," or "ability," reinforcing that an ability is a power. The gifts of the Spirit are *dynamis*. This word is used in Acts 1:8 describing it as such:

> But you will receive power when the Holy Spirit comes on you; and you will be my witnesses in Jerusalem, and in all Judea and Samaria, and to the ends of the Earth. (NIV)

Exousia is a Greek word meaning power of authority often linked with power of government rule, which others must obey. The translation of this word in the 21st Century King James version of the Bible as "power" may make the meaning a bit muddled.

Behold, I give unto you <u>power</u> to tread on serpents and scorpions and over all the power of the enemy, and nothing shall by any means hurt you. (Luke 10:19 KJ21)

The first word translated "power" is from *exousia*. Using authority in the place of power brings clarity to where the power comes from in order for us to conquer the works of the enemy. Jesus gives us His authority and He supplies the power to enforce it. Where did Jesus get this authority? Why does He have it?

To really understand what authority God has given us we need to go back farther than the beginning of humankind. We need to first establish a basic understanding of God and Heaven. Many verses in the Bible show that these two are different from Earth in two major ways:

1. The flow of time.
2. The substance of their being.

Time and Space

<u>For a thousand years in Your sight are like yesterday when it is past</u>, or as a watch in the night. (Psalms 90:4)

> Nevertheless, do not let this one fact escape your notice, beloved, that with the Lord <u>one day is like a thousand years, and a thousand years is like one day.</u> (2 Peter 3:8)

From this verse, it is clear that, where time is concerned, Heaven is using a different frame of reference than the standard used on Earth. At first glance, Peter seems to contradict himself. Intellectually we can accept that a day here on Earth is equivalent to a thousand years in Heaven, but what about the second half of that quote? Peter also says that a thousand years here is like a day in Heaven.

This contradiction is so perplexing that many people ignore it completely focusing on half that seems more plausible to them: the math. This verse is stating that 1,000=1 and 1=1,000. Most of us can do the math and figure out that if one equals 1,000 then our one is really 1/1000. This is just a new fact. But when we also state our 1,000 is equal to the Lord's one then that's asking us to believe there is no constant parallel between the two. For this reason, people tend to do one of two things:

KEYS TO AUTHORITY FOR EVERY BELIEVER

1. Dismiss the last part of that sentence
2. Reverse the order of the implied objects so that the second half of the statement is just repeating what was already stated.

These rationalizations are understandable but in error. For us, time is a constant, a finite, solid, and unchangeable fact. It is hard to imagine life without that binding force.

By ignoring the totality of the surrounding passages, we overlook the actual intent of the entire quotation. The word "like" is usually used for a comparison to show similarities. Here it is used twice in exact opposite ways creating a stark contrast defining time as it is in Heaven. When taken as a whole, it seems clear that the Holy Spirit, through Peter, is saying that time is not a binding force for God in Heaven as it is on Earth. This can be seen by the context surrounding this verse.

The chapter opens with Peter sharing the words of the prophets—men and women who foretold future events. Peter then reminds us that God created the Earth and, by the power of His mere words, reserved it for destruction until judgment day. Combined, these two statements show God's dominion over time and events. Then Peter makes his contradicting comparison that shows how vastly different time is to God and in Heaven after which he begs his audience not to lose hope.

> The Lord does not delay [as though He were unable to act] and is not slow about His promise, as some count slowness, but is [extraordinarily] patient toward you, not wishing for any to perish but for all to come to repentance. (2 Peter 3:9)

Taken as a whole, the first part of this chapter not only shows that the measure of time is different in Heaven, but that God is not limited by it.

If you think about the pure physics of what the Bible tells us about Heaven and what we know about Earth, this makes perfect sense. The flow of time on Earth is measured by how the planet spins on its axis and travels around the sun. Heaven has no sun or moon for a light source.

> And the city has no need of the sun nor of the moon to give light to it, for the glory (splendor, radiance) of God has illumined it… (Revelation 21:23)

> And there will be no night there. And they need no lamp, or light of the sun; for the Lord God gives them light. (Revelation 22:5)

Without a sun to revolve around there would be no way to measure time. Would time even exist as we know it? In recent years, the number of people going to Heaven and returning is increasing. This is evidenced by the sheer number of biographies that have been published in the last decade by Christian authors including those of Todd Burpo, Judy Franklin, Jeramy Nelson, Robert Henderson, Kevin Zadai, Kevin Basconi, and Akiane Kramarik. Those who have visited our future home say it feels like weeks instead of minutes or even seconds. Others say though they were gone for hours, weeks or days, it seemed like minutes. Every account speaks of the brightness of Heaven and the lack of darkness and night.

In a place that has never needed a sun or moon, where all things are eternal and never die, why should we expect time to flow the same as it does on Earth in such a place? It's a shortsighted notion and vain of beings who themselves are so restricted by time.

How about God who rules Heaven and Earth? (Psalms 103:19, Colossians 1:16) The Bible tells us that He existed before time and created the heavens and the Earth. (Genesis 1:1, John 1:1-2) Furthermore, it tells us that

God doesn't just exist eternally and throughout time, He inhabits it.

> Before the mountains were born or before You had given birth to the Earth and the world, even from everlasting to everlasting, You are [the eternal] God. (Psalms 90:2)

> For the high and exalted One, He who inhabits eternity, whose name is Holy says this... (Isaiah 57:14)

The Hebrew word for "inhabits" is *shakan,* meaning to abide in, dwell. This is a present tense word, not past tense. Which means that God is, right now, dwelling in all forms of time. This explains why He knows the end at the beginning: He is at the end right now as well as in the current time. (For information about how this affects our free will, see "Why Doesn't God Speak to Me?")

Eternal, by definition is without a beginning or an end; it means boundless. Is not time a limitation? Therefore, time cannot affect God; He is not limited by time. This concept became very clear to me when an established man of God, let's call him John, relayed an event that occurred in his life.

Time Travel

Through a series of miraculous events, John left a well-paying corporate job in Texas to follow the calling of God. Among other things, this meant a drastic cut in his income. He worked hard at listening to God and trying to do what He would have him do. Early in the life of his ministry, John set out to lead a group on a tour of Israel. He spoke about this event on a TV show that I found online. The following excerpt from my book, "Why Doesn't God Speak to Me?" describes John's experience.

One week before John was to leave to guide a group on a trip in Israel, his business partner, who was handling the finances and travel arrangements, left town and took all the money the people had given for their trip with him. John felt God wanted him to do the responsible thing and make good on the promise that was given to the twenty-two people who had trusted him with their money so he took out a loan for $50,000 to pay for the promised trip.

Back in the 1980s, this was more than three times his annual income. Because of this, John was quite irritated and not acting very godly as they visited Jerusalem. That night two angels appeared beside his bed. Each angel grabbed one of his arms as they said, "The Lord has need of you, come with us."

John looked back over his shoulder as he was being hauled bodily from the room. His wife lay asleep on the bed—his body was not next to hers. He knew that this was actually happening to his physical body, it was not an out-of-body experience.

The two angels took him through the hotel wall, and time and space bent around John, as it seemed like they were traveling hundreds of miles per hour. With a thud, he landed on a street paved with stones. The first thing that hit him was the smell. John had only been queasy once in his life, but the intense odor of animals and their feces mixed with overpowering human body odor was enough to gag him—he thought surely he would die from the stench alone.

Gone were the pajamas he was wearing; now John was dressed in robes that reached down to his sandaled feet. A corded belt held the robes together. He knew instantly that he was on Market Street in Jerusalem in the time of David. He also knew that he had to go up one side of the street and tell everyone three things: Saul's reign would soon end, David would be the next king, and David would restore Israel to greatness again.

Not knowing what else to do, John went to the first person and relayed what God had told him. Even though he thought in English, when he spoke it came out in Hebrew. When the person responded, he heard them speaking in Hebrew, but understood in English what they were saying. He received many types of answers. Some said, "Yes, yes, we know, Saul killed thousands and David killed tens of thousands" or "long live King David!" Some people asked if he was a prophet and wanted to talk to him, but he quickly excused himself and got on with the job God assigned to him.

While making his way from person to person, John's thoughts were going wild: How will I support myself here? I could be a carpenter... but do they even have saws yet? What will my wife do? I will be "that pastor who deserted the tour group in Israel in the middle of the night!" She won't be able to collect life insurance... how will she support herself?

All this went through his head as he did what he knew was his job from God. As he neared the end of the street, across the way was a small auburn-haired young man. A golden glow surrounded him that extended out by about eight inches. The young man motioned toward him, "Come here!"

John looked around and quickly realized that the soon-to-be-king was addressing him. David approached him and they met in the middle of the street where a cart being pulled by a donkey passed them by. David had dark auburn, wavy hair and a face that would be the envy of any male model. He stood less than five-feet tall and probably weighed one hundred pounds at the most.

David took John's hands in his own tiny, child-size hands and said, "I know whom you are and I know why you are here and I will see you again."

When the future king released his hands, John was whisked again through time and space. He landed in his jammies on his bed, bouncing with the force. His wife woke and mumbled, "Do you feel the presence of God here...it is so strong!"

The next morning, John reluctantly shared what happened with his tour group. He said they looked at him in fear, like they were sure he was a cult leader. Their tour guide arrived a short time later. He was very excited and insisted, "There is a brand-new exhibit, first time ever to be seen here in Jerusalem. We must go there."

The tour group wanted to go; reluctantly John agreed to see that instead of a unique site in the Holy Land, Magdala. At the lowest level of the exhibit was the newly unearthed Market Street from the time of David—it looked exactly as John described it. The group was convinced that John's trip was real.

I had heard and believed that all things are possible for God (Matthew 19:26, Job 42:2, Jeremiah 32:17), but this story really shed a whole new light on how easy things are for God. It literally blew away the boundaries on what God could or could not do. Not only did God whisk John through time and space and without the help of a time machine disguised as a phone booth à la "Doctor Who"; He changed John's clothes while he was in transit.

If we are to learn anything from this transaction it is that we must not apply our limited concepts of time and space to Him. He is operating on a level so far above us that even with the technological advances of a 21st century society, we are merely glimpsing at an iota of the vast chasm that lies between us and Him.

1st Key
Time & Space

Time and space do not restrict God's limitless power. The Bible says all things are easy for God (Genesis 18:1). This is a basic foundational Christian belief necessary to understand our authority.

THE REALM OF THE SPIRIT

Jesus declared that God is a spirit being.

<u>God is a Spirit</u>: and they that worship Him must worship in spirit and truth. (John 4:24)

Since Jesus was God's Son, He should know what exactly God is. Since God is a spirit being, and we know that He lives in Heaven, sometimes mentioned as "heavens," the logical assumption is that Heaven is a spirit realm or dimension. The Bible constantly refers to it as the "unseen" or "invisible" realm. It is a place we cannot contact with our natural physical senses.

God is a tripartite: a three-part being— Father, Son, and Holy Spirit. We were created in the image or "like" God. (Genesis 1:26) We have three parts to our being:

> ➤ Spirit – our inner being that is like God. Most times we are unable to see or feel this part of our being with our natural bodies.
> ➤ Soul – our mind, will, and emotions
> ➤ Body – our physical selves

In the Bible, "man" is often used in the genderless sense, meaning all of human kind. In this context our spirit is referred to as our "inner man" or our "heart." God is a spirit, and like Him, this is the part of humanity that lives forever. In scripture, Paul confirms that we are this tripartite:

> Now may the God of peace himself sanctify you completely, and may your whole spirit and soul and body be kept blameless at the coming of our Lord Jesus Christ. (1 Thessalonians 5:23)

It is instinctive to put that which you can see and feel at the top of the list in order of power, however, that would be wrong. Are we

18

more powerful than God? The part of us that is like God is the most powerful part of our beings.

> By faith we understand that the worlds were framed by the word of God, so that <u>the things which are seen were not made of things which are visible.</u> (Hebrews 11:3 NKJV)

All things were created by God from the spirit realm. Which is greater: the thing that *is* created or that *from which* something is formed? Thanks to movies and television shows, we think of spirit beings as ghosts, insubstantial and most times ineffectual in the physical realm. The spirit realm is portrayed as dismal, indistinct, and unsubstantial.

This couldn't be farther from the truth. Angels are spirit beings created by God to be His servants. Each person has a guardian angel (Psalm 91:11, Hebrews 1:14) and other angels visit the Earth as directed by God. People are dazzled by the spirit beings appearance when they fully reveal themselves. After all, it was two angels disguised as men who destroyed the cities of Sodom and Gomorrah. (Genesis 19)

Paul has given the correct hierarchy for our beings in his writing. The spirit is the most powerful, followed by the soul (the mind, will, and emotions). The body goes along with whichever of the other two beings is stronger.

> ...yet for us there is but one God, the Father, who is the source of all things... (1 Corinthians 8:6)

This is another verse that refers to the fact that the physical world was made from the unseen (the spirit). Therefore, the spirit realm can affect and even have the power to create new things in the physical world.

Reportedly, the spirit realm is more vast and powerful than the physical world. Every account given of a visit to Heaven seems to agree that the spirit realm is more multi-layered and ultra-real than the physical world with which we are familiar. The Bible tells us it is where those who recognize Jesus as Lord will go when they die.

> For indeed Christ died for sins once for all, the Just and Righteous for the unjust and unrighteous [the innocent for the guilty] so that He might bring us to God, having been put to death in the flesh, but made alive in the Spirit... (1 Peter 3:18)

According to all versions of the Bible, there are several areas of Heaven. For example, the first and the third Heavens are referenced in the sacred text; the third Heaven is where God lives and the first Heaven is the atmosphere around the Earth. We will discuss more about this subject in the forthcoming *Believers' Boot Camp* book, "Roadmap to Heaven." The system God created for us to grow and develop in is the physical, natural world. Because of this, substantial bodies are necessary to interact with it. Our physical existence is riddled with limitations involving both time and space. Could it be, for instance, that the entire point of this life is to prepare us all for the afterlife and eternity?

The Bible speaks of crowns given for work completed here on Earth (2 Timothy 4:8, 1 Corinthians 9:25, James 1:12, 1 Peter 5:2-4), and that there is treasure stored up in Heaven for what is done here (Matthew 6:19-20). It also speaks of tests and trials that we are given, which we may pass or fail. Thus, it's not unrealistic to assume that the results of a test must have some significant purpose.

Mere logic tells us it wouldn't make sense to give humans supernatural powers and let them into Heaven if they hadn't first developed a healthy respect for God and his ways here on Earth. What kind of Heaven would that be with indestructible beings potentially killing, stealing, or destroying things?

The purpose of living in this temporary and limited realm is to prepare for an eternity with God. Once we become aware of the two opposing and eternal kingdoms, it is time to choose which side we want to be on. Now that we know about time and space, eternity, and the difference between the spiritual and physical worlds, we can begin to explore our authority and from where it comes.

2nd Key
Spiritual Realm

Everything came from the spiritual realm called Heaven. This means that the spiritual world can affect our physical reality.

22

God Gives Authority

God is a spirit who lives in an unseen realm most of us cannot yet access (The FREE book, "Roadmap to Heaven," will explain how and why that is changing.) He created Earth and the Heavens. He created the stars, moon, sun, and the entire universe.

Now that you know how differently time works and the power of the spiritual realm, you may find it helpful to think of the universe as if it is encapsulated in a sphere; a creation enclosed and protected with rules put into place by its Creator. After God created the world and it was complete and perfect He said:

Let Us [Father, Son, and Holy Spirit] make mankind in Our image, after Our likeness, and <u>let them have complete authority</u> over the fish of the sea, the birds of the air, the [tame] beasts, and over all of the Earth, and over everything that creeps upon the Earth. So God created man in His own image, in the image and likeness of God He created him; male and female He created them. (Genesis 1:1-27)

The system God designed, He gave to mankind. Adam and Eve were appointed caretakers of Earth and everything on it. It is important to note that God placed the authority upon spirits who had physical bodies. This was the system He created. What God gives, He does not take back.

> God is not a man, that He should tell or act a lie, neither the son of man, that He should feel repentance or compunction [for what He has promised]. Has He said and shall He not do it? Or has He spoken and shall He not make it good? (Numbers 23:19)

> My covenant will I not break or profane, nor alter the thing that is gone out of My lips. (Psalms 89:34)

The Hebrew word *bĕriyth* translated as "covenant" means divine ordinance with signs or pledges. God spoke, it came out from His lips and was the first agreement between God and man. This was the original design to the system of authority on the Earth.

Let's say you give someone a pearl-white Cadillac with gold trim and they decide to paint flames on the hood, add big fenders, a five-inch lift, and fuzzy dice that dangle from the rear-view mirror. Would it be fair to tell them, "You are ruining it!" and take the car back just because you don't like what they've done to it? God is just and fair, when He gives something,

He gives it unconditionally and doesn't take it back. God gave the title deed of the Earth to man to do with it as we desired.

SATAN STEALS AUTHORITY

Knowing more about your enemy increases your chance of success in any battle. Why does Satan hate us? Why did he want the authority given to man? There is no book in the Bible dedicated to Satan, but he is certainly mentioned, and if you look for it, you can find much about our enemy in the Word of God.

The Kingdom of Heaven is organized much like our world. ("Why Doesn't God Speak to Me?" explains why.) God created Lucifer; he was a servant and an angel working for God.

> How you have fallen from heaven, O star of the morning [light-bringer], son of the dawn! (Isaiah 14:12)

The name "Lucifer" comes from the King James translation of the Bible. The Hebrew word *heylel*, meaning "light-bringer or shining one," was also translated from Latin to mean "morning star." Lucifer was the most beautiful being that God had created at that point in time.

> You had the full measure of perfection and the finishing touch [of completeness], full of wisdom and perfect in beauty. (Ezekiel 28:13)

Perhaps you have heard the saying, "Pride comes before a fall." The actual scripture reads:

> "Pride goes before destruction, and an haughty spirit before a fall." (Proverbs 16:18)

Likely this was the origin of that saying. Lucifer was beautiful, and he became proud and arrogant because of it.

> Your heart was proud and arrogant because of your beauty; you destroyed your wisdom for the sake of your splendor. (Ezekiel 28:17)

Lucifer decided that he was too good to serve, that he instead should be served.

> But you said in your heart, "I will ascend to Heaven; I will raise my throne above the stars of God; I will sit on the mount of assembly in the remote parts of the north. I will ascend above the heights of the clouds; I will make myself like the Most High." (Isaiah 14:13-14)

The Bible is the inspired word of God—every word is accurate. Ancient Hebrew used in the origin text is like all languages, there are many definitions for every word. It is often helpful to go back to the original words and take a second look if something doesn't make sense in our common language of today. Let us look at some other definitions for the words used for "above the stars of God."

Above - ma`al - above them, over

The stars - kowkab - shining

Of God - 'el - God-like, mighty ones, angels

The Hebrew word *'el* is most often translated as "of God." However, this doesn't mean it should always be translated that way. This passage should be read: "above them (those) shining god-like, mighty angels." Lucifer wanted to be above the other angels of God. He wanted to be in a higher place of authority. When man was created, he saw a way to get that authority.

> What is man that You are mindful of him, and the son of [earthborn] man that You care for him? Yet You have made him a little lower than God, and You have crowned him with glory and honor. You made him to have dominion over the works of Your hands; You have put all things under his feet... (Psalms 8:4-6)

Man was created as a child of God. Angels were servants of God. Who has more authority? You know that must have irritated Lucifer when man was placed above him.

When Adam and Eve disobeyed God, they placed themselves under the authority of the spirit they obeyed, Lucifer. Our Bible does not mention Lucifer in the garden by name, only as a snake. However, "Thayer's English-Greek Lexicon of the New Testament"[i] says that the serpent was an emblem of cunning and wisdom to ancient Hebrews—they regard the snake as the Devil himself. Referring to evil people as snakes is prevalent throughout the Bible. For instance, crafty hypocrites are called serpents in the Book of Matthew. And the Book of Ezekiel confirms Lucifer was in Eden.

> You were in Eden, the garden of God; every precious stone was your covering… You were an anointed guardian cherub. (Ezekiel 28:13-14)

Many people dismiss this verse because Ezekiel was told to say these things to the King of Tyre. It has been argued that these pertain to a physical kingdom and a physical king. However, no physical king was in the Garden of Eden.

What many fail to realize is that there is more than one type of ruler: physical and spiritual. Lucifer is an angel; he is not omnipresent like God. He cannot be everywhere at once so he needs a ruling body akin to what we have in the physical Earth:

> For our struggle is not against flesh and blood [contending only with physical opponents], but against the <u>rulers</u>, against <u>the powers</u>, against the world <u>forces of this [present] darkness</u>, against the <u>spiritual forces of wickedness in the heavenly (supernatural) places.</u> (Ephesians 6:2)

There are spiritual rulers including spiritual kings ruling over physical areas. Daniel, who survived being thrown into a den of lions, gives an example of this. Daniel had sought an answer from God for weeks as he fasted and prayed. When an angel appeared before Daniel the rest of the men could not see him, but felt the presence of the powerful being and ran, leaving Daniel alone with the heavenly messenger. (Daniel 10:1-9)

> Then he said to me, "Do not be afraid, Daniel, for from the first day that you set your heart on understanding this and on humbling yourself before your God, your words were heard, and I have come

in response to your words. But the <u>prince of the kingdom of Persia</u> was standing in opposition to me for twenty-one days. Then, behold, Michael, one of the chief [of the celestial] princes, came to help me, for I had been left there with the <u>kings of Persia</u>." (Daniel 10 12-13)

The Archangel Michael wouldn't have needed to come and help if Gabriel was merely contending with the physical kings of Persia. Gabriel was speaking about the spiritual kings, a ruler in the spiritual realm over a city.

Son of man, take up a dirge (funeral poem to be sung) for the king of Tyre and say to him, "Thus says the Lord God, You had the full measure of perfection and the finishing touch [of completeness], full of wisdom and perfect in beauty. <u>You were in Eden, the garden of God</u>…" (Ezekiel 28:12-13)

Here Ezekiel was speaking of the spiritual King of Tyre because only a spiritual being could have been alive at the time of the creation of Eden. This entire passage in Ezekiel is about Lucifer, which confirms his presence in Eden.

After this incident in the Garden, Lucifer earns the name Satan in the Old Testament. This word means "adversary, in a legal setting."

Once mankind was forced to leave the Garden of Eden, the Bible states that Satan is god of this world (2 Corinthians 4:4, John 12:31, 1 John 5:19). Note that lowercase "g" denotes not the one true God, but a being more powerful than man.

This was the state of the Earth when Jesus came. Sin became a part of every man, who would be born with flaws and thus would move farther away from God. This was a considerable coup for Satan. Remember the system in place: you must have a body to exert authority on Earth. Now, every person was born with the ability to do both good and evil and authority had been given to our enemy.

When man follows his sinful nature, or that which is opposed to the teachings of God, authority is given to the spirit being obeyed—Satan. The only authority Satan has is that which is given to him by physical beings on Earth. But with sin being a part of every man from conception, Satan has easy access to mankind making him the new god of this world.

> Yet death ruled [over mankind] from Adam to Moses [the Lawgiver], even over those who had not sinned as Adam did. Adam is a type of Him (Christ) who

was to come [but in reverse—Adam brought destruction, Christ brought salvation]. (Romans 5:14)

Do you need to teach a boy how to desire having sex with a girl (outside marriage)? Do you need to teach a child how to lie? To both questions the answer is no, they just do. Pride, arrogance, hate, and so much more are characteristics with which we are born.

…for all have sinned and fall short of the glory of God… (Romans 3:23 NIV)

JESUS TAKES AUTHORITY BACK

Things were pretty bleak for thousands of years. But there was also good news. In fact, the gospel (the story of the coming of Jesus and the Kingdom of God) is literally the English translation from Greek meaning "the good news." God, in his great love for us, had a backup plan from the beginning of time.

God is omnipotent and can do anything, but this doesn't mean that He will do *anything*. He put rules in place and now has to abide by them. God needed a man on Earth to take back what Satan had tricked Adam and Eve into giving up. It would take another spirit in a physical body to get that authority back.

God gave Jesus a human body so that through His obedience unto death, He could take back all authority under Heaven and Earth.

> Hence, when He [Christ] entered into the world, He said, "Sacrifices and offerings You have not desired, but instead You have made ready a body for Me [to offer]…" (Hebrews 10:5)

> So then as through one trespass [Adam's sin] there resulted condemnation for all men, even so through one act of righteousness there resulted justification of life to all men. For just as through one man's disobedience [his failure to hear, his carelessness] the many were made sinners, so through the obedience of the one Man the many will be made righteous and acceptable to God and brought into right standing with Him. (Romans 5:18-19)

This is why we are commanded to spread the word through the Gospel about what Jesus accomplished on Earth. After Jesus died and rose from the dead three days later, He took back the authority that originally belonged to Adam and Eve.

Jesus came up and said to them, "<u>All authority</u> (all power of absolute rule) in Heaven and on Earth has been given to Me." (Matthew 28:18)

I have <u>given you authority</u> to trample on snakes and scorpions and to overcome all the power of the enemy; nothing will harm you. (Luke 10:19 NIV)

Jesus did what Adam didn't do: He was obedient to God, even if it meant enduring a torturous death. By doing this, He took back the authority from Satan. As a result, not only are we given the opportunity to go to Heaven because of what Jesus did, but He has given us His authority to use here on Earth.

For <u>it is by grace</u> [God's remarkable compassion and favor drawing you to Christ] that you have been saved [actually delivered from judgment and given eternal life] <u>through faith</u>. And this [salvation] is not of yourselves [not through your own effort], but it is the [undeserved, gracious] gift of God… (Ephesians 2:8)

There is no distinction, since all have sinned and continually fall short of the glory of God, and are being justified [declared free of the guilt of sin, made acceptable to God, and granted eternal life] as a <u>gift by His [precious, undeserved] grace</u>, through the redemption [the payment for our sin], which is [provided] in Christ Jesus... (Romans 3:22-24)

Jesus made a way for us to enter Heaven, not on our own merits but because of His right standing (righteousness) with God on our behalf. Now that He has gone to Heaven, and is seated at the right hand of God, He brings with Him those who honor Him as Lord. This is seen in the following passages.

Inasmuch then as we [believers] <u>have a great High Priest who has [already ascended and] passed through the heavens,</u> Jesus the Son of God, let us hold fast our confession [of faith and cling tenaciously to our absolute trust in Him as Savior]. (Hebrews 4:14)

So then, when the Lord Jesus had spoken to them, <u>He was taken up into Heaven and sat down at the right hand of God.</u> (Mark 16:19)

This occurred after Jesus died and was buried in a tomb. On the third day, He rose again, and over the next few weeks He spoke to hundreds of people. His eleven disciples would later witness the Son of God being taken up into Heaven.

But God, being [so very] rich in mercy, because of His great and wonderful love with which He loved us, even when we were [spiritually] dead and separated from Him because of our sins, He made us [spiritually] alive together with Christ (for by His grace—His undeserved favor and mercy—you have been saved from God's judgment). And He raised us up together with Him [when we believed], and seated us with Him in the heavenly places, [because we are] in Christ Jesus. (Ephesians 2:4-6)

This is why acknowledging the connection between the spirit, mind, and body are so important. The spirit realm is so different from what we know. The Bible tells us that after we accept Jesus as Lord we are seated with Him in heavenly places.

In a society ruled by a king, not unlike Heaven, being seated next to the sovereign ruler is a place of power and authority. Angels are servants of God, and we are children of God. Angels must stand in His presence; we are seated.

But to which of the angels has the Father ever said, "Sit at My right hand [together with me in royal dignity], until I make your enemies a footstool for your feet [in triumphant conquest]?" (Hebrews 1:13)

And He <u>has put all things under His feet</u>...
(Ephesians 1:22)

God will make Jesus' enemies a footstool, under His feet. We are seated with Jesus, in a place of power. What exact position do we hold? We must keep reading in Ephesians to find out:

...and has <u>appointed Him the universal and supreme Head of the church</u> [a headship exercised throughout the church] <u>Which is His body</u>, the fullness of Him Who fills all in all [for in that body lives the full measure of Him Who makes everything complete, and Who fills everything everywhere with Himself].
(Ephesians 1:22-23)

Jesus is at the top – He is the Head, our Leader, and our Lord. The Church is His body. This means we need to wait for instructions from the Head before we act.

Would we want our hand to be doing something our head didn't tell it to do? Would we want our mouth to start declaring things any time it wants to? In the natural world we would call this Tourette's Syndrome, a disorder that isn't any fun to have.

How do we receive orders from our Head, the Lord? He has given us a Comforter, Guide, a Counselor, the Holy Spirit.

But the Comforter, which is the Holy Ghost, whom the Father will send in my name, he shall teach you all things… (John 14:26)

Howbeit when He, the Spirit of truth, is come, He will guide you into all truth: for He shall not speak of himself; but whatsoever He shall hear, that shall he speak: and He will shew you things to come.

The Holy Spirit is our Guide. Jesus said He **only** did what He saw His Father doing. We are to be like Jesus. It is the Holy Spirit who reveals what is going on in Heaven, what God is saying and what we need to do.

For as many as are led by the Spirit of God, they are the sons of God. (Romans 8:14)

We need to let the Holy Spirit lead every prayer. Then our words will be filled with Him and His power. This is what enables us to speak like Jesus did and "call things that are not as if they were." (Romans 4:17)

3rd Key
Holy Spirit

We are seated in Jesus at the right hand of God, a place of power and authority. He is the Head and we are His body. We must listen for instructions from our Head, which come from the Holy Spirit. Then we can rest assured that it will be done.

How to Get Authority

And He said to them, "Go into all the world and preach the gospel to all creation. He who has believed [in Me] and has been baptized will be saved [from the penalty of God's wrath and judgment]; but he who has not believed will be condemned. These signs will accompany <u>those who have believed</u>: <u>in My name they will cast out demons</u>, they will speak in new tongues; they will pick up serpents, and if they drink anything deadly, it will not hurt them; they will lay hands on the sick, and they will get well." (Mark 16:15-18)

Those who believe and are "baptized" will receive salvation. This is one of the verses from where we get the expression "being saved." It is a way of saying we have received salvation. Contrary to what some may assume, baptism has its roots in Jewish history; John the Baptist didn't invent it.

In ancient times, if you married a Jewish person and wanted to convert and become part of the Jewish community, Gentiles (those not born Jewish) would be taught about God, confess that He is God, then be dunked underwater. This was symbolic of the act of shedding an old life and becoming a new creation, one of God's people. In the "Mishneh Torah," the code by which the Jewish people live, it gives instruction to immerse all "unclean" things in water be it human or otherwise. Jesus spoke about baptism in this way:

> I assure you and most solemnly say to you, <u>unless a person is born again [reborn from above—spiritually transformed</u>, renewed, sanctified], he cannot [ever] see and experience the Kingdom of God. (John 3:3)

If you have been asked if you are a born-again believer, this is what they are referring to. It is a spiritual transformation. Jesus and His disciples showed us that believing isn't enough. Even the demons know that He is the Son of God and tremble at His name. (James 2:19) There must be a conversion within. We must submit our will to someone we cannot see, Jesus.

JESUS IS LORD

> …because <u>if you acknowledge and confess with your mouth that Jesus is Lord</u> [recognizing His power, authority, and majesty as God], and <u>believe in your heart</u> that God raised Him from the dead, you will be saved. For with the heart a person believes [in Christ

as Savior] resulting in his justification [that is, being made righteous—being freed of the guilt of sin and made acceptable to God]; and with the mouth he acknowledges and confesses [his faith openly], resulting in and confirming [his] salvation. (Romans 10:9-10)

This is another verse that speaks more clearly about "being saved." Once we acknowledge Jesus as Lord and believe in our hearts, we receive salvation. This is not an act that should be done lightly. The word "lord" means owner: a landlord is the landowner. It can also mean hereditary right or preeminence to whom that service and obedience is due. By taking Jesus as Lord you are saying that you will serve and obey Him.

Several places in the Bible refer to those who have taken Jesus as Lord as "bondservants." These are willing slaves to a master. If you had a debt you could not pay, you could go to jail or you could willingly become a bondservant until the debt was paid.

This means we agree to do things His way, not our way, to put Him first in all matters. It makes perfect sense that Jesus only gives authority to those who are under His command, doesn't it? If you have not yet accepted Jesus as your Lord, owner and Savior—your only way into Heaven—it is simple to do so.

Saying the words is easy, but meaning them is what truly matters. The thief who hung on the cross next to Jesus made this simple statement, "Jesus, remember me when You come into your Kingdom." Because he believed what he was saying, that was enough for the thief to be forgiven and see Jesus in Heaven. It is a matter of what you firmly believe, beyond any doubt, and that which you must heartily proclaim with words. To take Jesus as Lord, declare the following out loud:

Dear God,

I believe that Jesus Christ is the only begotten Son of God, that He came down to our Earth in the flesh and died on the cross to pay for all of my sins. I believe that Jesus rose from the dead on the third day to allow us to receive eternal life.

I accept You, Jesus as my personal Lord and Savior. I declare today that I will turn from all my sins in my life and I thank you that your blood blots them out from all records in Heaven and Earth.

I ask that You send the Holy Spirit to lead and guide me and to become one with my spirit, making me a new creation. I receive you Holy Spirit. Thank you for filling me to overflowing. Holy Spirit, please guide me and reveal to me any sins that remain in my life so that I can turn from them. I desire to live according to God's way from now on.

If you believe what you say and mean it with your whole heart, then you are under the protection and blessing of Jesus and His authority is available to you. This is the most important key to your authority.

If you cannot yet say this prayer and believe it with your whole heart, begin reading the books of the Bible: Matthew, Mark, Luke, and John in the New Testament. Before you begin, ask God to grant you wisdom and reveal Jesus to you. Come back and say this prayer when you KNOW these things to be so with all your heart.

4th Key
Jesus is Lord

Taking Jesus as Lord is the first and primary key to all authority. Our authority comes through Jesus, without Him we have no authority.

Without Jesus

It would be irresponsible of me to mention demons and casting them out without repeating the biblical warnings given about this. The story is so vivid and so graphic that there could be nothing better than to read it straight from the source.

> Then some of the traveling Jewish exorcists also attempted to call the name of the Lord Jesus over those who had evil spirits, saying, "I implore you and solemnly command you by the Jesus whom Paul preaches!" Seven sons of one [named] Sceva, a Jewish chief priest, were doing this. But the evil spirit retorted, "I know and recognize and acknowledge Jesus, and I know about Paul, but as for you, who are you?" Then the man, in whom was the evil spirit, leaped on them and subdued all of them and overpowered them, so that they ran out of that house [in terror, stripped] naked and wounded. (Acts 19:13-15)

This man didn't know Jesus as Lord. He tried to get rid of a demon by calling on the "Jesus that Paul knows." This is further evidence that you must have a relationship with Jesus to use the authority His name provides.

What was the result of this attempt to exert authority that had not been given? The demon-possessed man beat him and stole his clothes and chased him naked through the streets.

It is important to note that you develop a reputation in the spiritual realm. Word gets around if you are exercising your authority. Spirits will become quiet around you for fear that you will cast them out. Start on yourself, your home, your family, and your business.

Once He is Lord, He gives us His name to use. What exactly does it mean when you say "in the name of...?" When you have permission to use someone's name, you are claiming their reputation and authority instead of your own, according to the "English Reports Annotated" (Pages 1505-2672) Songs have been sung about the Name of Jesus. What is so special about His name?

Let us look back at the life of Jesus to answer this question. Before He went to the cross, Jesus consistently said things like this:

I have come in <u>My Father's name</u>, and you do not receive Me… (John 5:43 NKJV)

I do <u>nothing on My own authority</u>, but I say these things <u>just as My Father taught Me</u>. (John 8:28)

Jesus did everything in His Father's authority, because man, at least at this time, had none. This is reflected in how He referred to Himself:

Do not tell anyone what you have seen until the <u>Son of Man</u> has been raised from the dead. (Matthew 17:9)

But so that you may know that the <u>Son of Man</u> has authority and the power on Earth to forgive sins… (Matthew 9:5)

These are two examples of what amounts to dozens of existing passages where Jesus refers to Himself as the "Son of man." The implication was that the things He did while on Earth were what man could do when appropriating the power and authority of God. He wasn't doing these acts as God, but as a man under the laws that had been established on Earth. After Jesus' crucifixion, however, everything changed. What formerly had been referred to as "My Father's" authority, became the following:

> Jesus came up and said to them, "All authority (all power of absolute rule) in Heaven and on Earth has <u>been given to Me.</u>" (Matthew 28:18)

Now instead of using His Father's authority, Jesus had been given His own. This is what makes His name so important. Through Paul, the Holy Spirit provides us with a little more insight into what this means:

> God has highly exalted Him and <u>bestowed on Him the name which is above every name</u>… (Philippians 2:9)

> …when He raised Him from the dead and <u>seated Him at His own right hand in the heavenly places, far above all rule and authority and power and dominion</u> [whether angelic or human], and [far above] <u>every name that is named</u> [above every title that can be conferred], not only in this age and world but also in the one to come. (Ephesians 1:20-21)

"Above" is the Greek word, *huperanō,* which means higher in rank or power. It isn't referring to being higher up in the air somewhere. When you are seated at the right hand of a ruler, it is a place of power. Jesus is seated at the right hand of God. This means He is above all power that is not seated in the same position.

One of the most powerful things Jesus did while on this Earth was to give us His name to use. This is why most prayers state, "In the name of Jesus." He himself said:

> Very truly I tell you, whoever believes in me will do the works I have been doing, and they will do even greater things than these, because I am going to the Father. <u>And I will do whatever you ask in my name</u>, so that the Father may be glorified in the Son. You may ask me for anything in my name, and I will do it. (John 14:12-14)

We must examine this whole section, not just the one line. Jesus is talking about us doing the same works that He was doing. What did He do?

> …the Son is able to do nothing of Himself (of His own accord); but <u>He is able to do only what He sees the Father doing</u>, for whatever the Father does is what the Son does in the same way…(John 5:19)

We are to follow His example: Do what we see the Father doing. This is when the Name of Jesus will carry the full weight and authority of the Kingdom. Have you prayed prayers in the Name of the King without Him telling you to do so? This may be why these prayers were not answered.

5th Key
The Name

The name of Jesus is a major key to your authority. In monarchies if in a particular matter you "come in the name of the king," you are stating that you have the authority of the king. Make sure you are doing as He wants by being led by the Spirit.

THE WORD OF GOD

Accepting Jesus as Lord will get you into Heaven. Clearly a significant benefit, being a believer will secure your eternity. But it does little for you here on Earth if you don't know how to use the authority the Lord gives you. Let us use the following scenario to explain this concept:

Amirah comes from an isolated part of the globe and has little information about much of the world's modern ways. Upon entering this country, she is given a wallet full of credit cards that have millions of dollars in value. With no instructions as to what they are for or how to use them, Amirah finds these small plastic cards are great for scraping ice off a windshield. She never realizes that everything she needed could be had with the proper use of her credit cards.

The Bible is our instruction book telling us about all the provisions God has for us. The Holy Spirit is our Guide to understanding it. Basic information on how to read and better understand the Bible can be found in my book, "Why Doesn't God Speak to Me?" We must be careful about demands and decrees even if we see it in the Bible.

> "Again I say to you that <u>if two of you agree</u> on earth concerning anything that they ask, it will be done for them by My Father in heaven." (Matthew 18:19 NKJV)

Many Christians quote this verse as they pray together. We sit with heads bowed, sometimes silently, sometimes with an "amen" to declare our agreement with what has been prayed. If God gave any two lunatics whatever the agreed upon, it would be chaos. Think about it in terms of a hot topic of today:

> Two people want President Trump dead… another two people don't like the Vice President's stance on a topic… we would quickly run out of leaders. There will NEVER be a leader that everyone likes. No one could stay in office long if God said yes to prayer of agreement by two people and removed a leader they were unhappy with.

Reading a bit further in the Bible you find there is a qualifying statement:

And this is the confidence that we have in him, that, if we ask <u>anything according to his will, he hears us</u>… (1 John 5:14 KJV)

Now this makes sense. God has a plan. When we search His word and listen to the Holy Spirit, then we know His ways and what He wants. Those are the prayers that get answered.

Reading the Bible, especially the gospels of Matthew, Mark, Luke, and John, is essential. By reading about the life of Jesus, we can better understand who God is in the human form of man.

When you read about the Lord it is important to remember that before He was crucified He addressed people under the Law of Moses—*The Ten Commandments*—and tried to get them to see that they needed a savior. You can tell when it is addressing people who are living according to Jewish laws and traditions because it will say, "if you do *this*, then God will do *that*." Under the new covenant, it will say, "because Jesus did *this*, now we can do *that*."

Jesus also says some things concerning the future, which apply to us today. Throughout the Bible it is important to know to whom the writer is speaking and why they are writing to this particular group. Knowing the context helps better understand what has been written.

Without the Gospel

Most of the time Jesus spoke in parables to the people. When He addressed the topic of casting out demons, it was one of the few times that He enlisted only a few metaphors with no chance of being misunderstood.

> Now when the unclean spirit has gone out of a man, it roams through waterless (dry, arid) places in search of rest, but it does not find it. Then it says, "<u>I will return to my house from which I came.</u>" And when it arrives, it finds the place unoccupied, swept, and put in order. Then it goes and brings with it seven other spirits more wicked than itself, and they go in and make their home there. And the last condition of that man becomes worse than the first. So will it also be with this wicked generation. (Matthew 12:43-45)

After casting out a demon, it may return "home." The Greek word for home is *oikos,* which means any dwelling place. In the case of demons, the home is the human body. If the body is tidy and put in order, in other words, under control or healed but vacant of the Holy

Spirit, demons can have access to us once again.

According to the Gospel, the Holy Spirit comes and lives inside us once we take Jesus as Lord. Without letting people know about Jesus and the benefit of the Holy Spirit, we could be doing more harm than good by attempting to get rid of a demon. The demon we cast out may return to the individual we freed and bring seven stronger allies with him to take control once more if a person does not have the Holy Spirit within them.

The word of God provides much knowledge and wisdom as well as power and authority. God wants us to use it to bring His kingdom to Earth. The more we learn, the more we can draw closer to Him, and the more effective we can be in our own lives.

6th Key
The Instruction Manual

The Bible shows us what authority we have and how to use it. It is important to read it and believe it, so that we can utilize the authority Jesus paid for with his own life on Earth.

The authority given to us through the death and resurrection of Jesus is one of the greatest weapons at our disposal, and yet it is not being employed by the Church as it should be.

As you begin to exercise your authority in your own home, your influence will grow. Demons knew of Paul and of Jesus; they fled their host when they were commanded to do so. (Acts 19:15) If you are called by the Lord to join the ministry, it may increase your realm of authority. But the blessing of authority begins in your home with your family. The Word gives us instructions in this:

> He must rule his own household well, keeping his children under control, with true dignity, commanding their respect in every way and keeping them respectful. For if a man does not know how to rule his own household, how is he to take care of the church of God? (1 Timothy 3:4-5)

Do you feel a calling of God in your life? It all begins at home. It is the most challenging battleground you will ever fight on, and the most important.

There are three main things that affect the authority Jesus gives us:

1. Obedience
2. Faith
3. Prayer and Fasting

Faith is a logical necessity. It is obedience that trips people up, so let's begin there.

Obedience

Many Christians will state that Jesus died for our sins and think that our obedience is no longer a factor. This couldn't be farther from the truth. Jesus freed us from the consequences of the Law of Moses, which the disciples refer to as the Law of Sin and Death. We no longer go to Hell when we sin because His sacrifice redeems us from the consequences of our sin. However, Jesus gave us a new law and He expects us to follow it.

> He who has My commandments and keeps them is the one who loves Me; and he who loves Me will be loved by My Father, and I will love him and will disclose Myself to him. (John 14:21 NKJV)

This is clearly stating that if we really believe that Jesus paid the ultimate price for us, it will inspire us to love Him. That if we love Him we will try our best to obey what He has

taught, and then He will reveal Himself to us.
What are the commandments of Jesus? After
accepting Him as Lord and as the only true
God, the trinity of Father, Son, and Holy Spirit,
there is only one commandment:

> I am giving you a new commandment, that you love
> one another. Just as I have loved you, so you too are
> to love one another. (John 13:34)

> And this is love: that we walk in accordance with His
> commandments and are guided continually by His
> precepts. This is the commandment, just as you have
> heard from the beginning, that you should [always]
> walk in love. (2 John 1:6)

This may sound like Jesus is the original
'70s hippie starting a revolution, but these are
His words and cannot be denied. On the
surface it sounds easy—to just love one
another like we love ourselves. The reality is
that this level of giving and kindness is
impossible to achieve without His help.

Let's not veer off on a tangent about love or
exactly what He expects. Jesus sent the Holy
Spirit to dwell inside us and guide us one small
step at a time. For this reason, someone who
has been walking with the Lord for many years
should have a deeper revelation and stronger

capacity for walking in love than a new Christian.

7th Key
Obedience

The key to remaining and increasing in authority is obedience. There is no magic formula, a magic phrase that we can use. Unlimited authority can only be achieved by following the guidance of the Holy Spirit. No need to leap into the deep end, if you let Him guide you one step at a time. Once you have, you will be shocked at how easy it is.

The Bible says, "as He is in this world so are we." (1 John 4:17) This is what the Word says about Jesus:

> And being found in human form, <u>he humbled himself by becoming obedient to the point of death</u>, even death on a cross. (Philippians 2:8 ESV)

Being obedient to someone else is humbling. It is saying that they know best, not you. Jesus was obedient and all authority was given to Him. The next verse confirms this:

> For this reason also [because He obeyed and so completely humbled Himself], God has highly exalted Him and bestowed on Him the name which is above every name, so that at the name of Jesus every knee shall bow [in submission], of those who are in Heaven and on Earth and under the Earth...
> (Philippians 2:9-10)

Due to His obedience, God elevated the name of Jesus higher (gave power over) raising it above all other names. Obedience matters. If we look closely at Jesus' life, we see an increase in authority. It is stated in the book of John:

> So Jesus answered them by saying, "I assure you and most solemnly say to you, the Son can do nothing of Himself [of His own accord], unless it is something He sees the Father doing; for whatever things the Father does, the Son [in His turn] also does in the same way. For the Father dearly loves the Son and shows Him everything that He Himself is doing; and the Father will show Him greater works than these,

<u>so that you will be filled with wonder</u>." (John 5:19-20)

Can you see the progression? First the Son does as He sees the Father doing, (revealed by the Holy Spirit) then the Father shows Him greater works so that people will be filled with wonder. Our obedience will bring more and more authority.

As He was in this world, so are we. (1 John 4:17)

Let's get one thing straight where obedience is concerned: it is important that you try your best, but don't stress out and condemn yourself about not doing everything exactly right. Jesus became human and knows how difficult life on Earth is. (Hebrews 2:18, 4:15, Philippians 2:6-8)

Paraphrasing John 1:9, he knows we can't be perfect and that is why He went to the cross as a sacrifice for our sins. God knows your heart, He really knows if you've tried to be obedient or if you're just giving Him lip service. If you mess up that is what Jesus died for: admit you missed a step and He will give you another chance like it never happened.

Talk with the Holy Spirit and He will guide you and show you how to do better. Don't try to go from zero to sixty in the blink of an eye. Take the steps the Holy Spirit has shown you. He will help you do it. But if you are not truly sorry for your wrongdoings or you don't really intend to cease your actions, He will know and respond accordingly. (Jeremiah 17:10, Acts 1:24, Romans 2:6) In the end, the choice is yours. If you choose not to learn more about God and be guided, there are consequences.

> Not everyone who says to Me, "Lord, Lord," will enter the Kingdom of Heaven, but only he who does the will of My Father who is in heaven. Many will say to Me on that day [when I judge them], "Lord, Lord, have we not prophesied in Your name, and driven out demons in Your name, and done many miracles in Your name?" And then I will declare to them publicly, "I never knew you; depart from Me [you are banished from My presence], you who act wickedly [disregarding My commands]." (Matthew 7:21-23)

The first mention of "kingdom" is the Greek word *basileia,* which refers to ruling power and place of authority, and insinuates the royal power and dignity conferred on Christians in the Messiah's kingdom. Researching verse twenty-three, at the urging of the Holy Spirit, led to a revelation about the meaning of the words translated "You who act wickedly." According to the *One New Man Bible* edited by Reverend William J. Morford, this phrase commonly means, "You who is without Torah (teaching) must depart from my presence."

Morford studied Hebrew under the grandson of the Eliezer Ben-Yehuda whose lifetime work was to make Modern Hebrew the national language of Israel. This version of the Bible includes a reference section where key aspects of the Hebrew culture and idioms of the time are explained.

When we put what we know about *basileia* and "you who act wickedly" together, it shows that some basic authority is given to every believer. It also shows that study and obedience are expected as you exercise your authority or there will be a limitation and a consequence. (The next book in the *Believer's Boot Camp* series will explain this further.)

You won't go to Hell for being disobedient. Your salvation is secure when you accept Jesus as Lord, but there are consequences in this life if you don't pursue knowledge of your Lord and follow what you learn with the honor He deserves.

Faith

What is faith? Faith is the concept of knowing that something is real even though you cannot see it.

> Now faith is the assurance (title deed, confirmation) of things hoped for (divinely guaranteed), and the evidence of things not seen [the conviction of their reality—faith comprehends as fact what cannot be experienced by the physical senses]. (Hebrews 11:1)

You use faith each and every day. In the natural world, faith is easy to understand. When you get into a car and push the radio's power button, you are placing your trust in a mechanical device to receive invisible airwaves and provide music within the vehicle—that is faith. You cannot see radio waves traveling through the air, but you believe that they are there.

Did you put on gravity boots this morning when you got out of bed? You had faith that an invisible force was present to keep you on the ground and prevent you from floating away. This is faith. You just KNOW that gravity exists, whether or not you see it. How do you get more faith?

So then faith cometh by hearing, and hearing by the Word of God. (Romans 10:17 KJ21)

Once you know that every Word of the Bible is inspired by the Holy Spirit, faith will come much easier. My book, "Why Doesn't God Speak to Me?" shares the scientific proof that validates the Bible as truth. It also gives some basic instruction on how to get the most out of reading the Word of God. Get a free copy of this book if you don't yet know about the amazing discoveries man has made concerning the Bible, or if you are struggling to understand what you read.

I have given many direct quotes from the Bible in this book because faith comes by hearing the Word of God. The act of familiarizing oneself with the words of the Bible will promote faith in readers. We need to *see* the actual words, think about them, and meditate upon them.

God has instructed us in His Word not to forsake the importance of assembling together. We are not under the Law of the Ten Commandments; our salvation is through Jesus. However, Paul puts it this way:

All things are lawful [that is, morally legitimate, permissible], but not all things are beneficial or advantageous. All things are lawful, but not all things are constructive [to character] and edifying [to spiritual life]. (1 Corinthians 10:23)

Going to Church is no longer a mandate that, if violated, will send us to Hell. But it is still beneficial. Jesus fulfilled the Law of Moses; also known as the law of sin and death and took care of the afterlife consequences for us. However assembling with other believers still profits us in this life.

One of the benefits about gathering together is that we get to hear God's word, both spoken and explained. This is in order that our faith can grow by hearing the Word and thinking about the meaning. If your church isn't giving you instruction and encouragement by quoting from the word of God, then pray for your pastor. If the circumstance doesn't change, find a new church.

The spoken Word of God is so very important. Everything God created in the first chapter of the Bible, He did by speaking words.

And God said, "Let there be light:" and there was light. (Genesis 1:3 ASV)

And <u>God said</u>, "Let there be an expanse in the midst of the waters, and let it separate the waters from the waters." (Genesis 1:6)

And <u>God said</u>, "Let the waters under the heavens be gathered together unto one place, and let the dry land appear:" and it was so. (Genesis 1:9 ASV)

And <u>God said</u>, "Let the <u>Earth</u> put forth grass, herbs yielding seed, and fruit-trees bearing fruit after their kind, wherein is the seed thereof, upon the <u>Earth</u>:" and it was so. (Genesis 1:11 ASV)

And <u>God said</u>, "Let there be lights in the firmament of heaven to divide the day from the night; and let them be for signs, and for seasons, and for days and years: and let them be for lights in the firmament of heaven to give light upon the Earth:" and it was so. (Genesis 1:14-15 ASV)

And <u>God said</u>, "Let the waters swarm with swarms of living creatures, and let birds fly above the Earth across the expanse of the heavens." (Genesis 1:20 ESV)

God even blessed the first humans using words:

And God blessed them: and God said unto them, "Be fruitful, and multiply, and replenish the Earth, and subdue it; and have dominion over the fish of the sea, and over the birds of the heavens, and over every living thing that moveth upon the Earth." (Genesis 1:28 ASV)

The old limerick, "Sticks and stones may break my bones, but words will never harm me," is opposite of what the Bible tells us:

"Death and life are in the power of the tongue, and those who love it and indulge it will eat its fruit and bear the consequences of their words." (Proverbs 18:21)

"But I tell you, on the day of judgment men will have to give account for every idle (inoperative, nonworking) word they speak. For by your words you will be justified and acquitted, and by your words you will be condemned and sentenced." (Matthew 12:36-37)

God's Word is important and so are our words. We are "like God." Not equal to, but similar to God. The Book of James teaches us how powerful the tongue is and it is worth reading what was written by inspiration of the Holy Spirit.

If we set bits in the horses' mouths to make them obey us, we can turn their whole bodies about. Likewise, look at the ships: though they are so great and are driven by rough winds, they are steered by a very small rudder wherever the impulse of the helmsman determines. Even so the tongue is a little member, and it can boast of great things. See how much wood or how great a forest a tiny spark can set ablaze! And the tongue is a fire. [The tongue is a] world of wickedness set among our members, contaminating and depraving the whole body and setting on fire the wheel of birth (the cycle of man's nature), being itself ignited by hell (Gehenna). For every kind of beast and bird, of reptile and sea animal, can be tamed and has been tamed by human genius (nature). But the human tongue can be tamed by no man. It is a restless (undisciplined, irreconcilable) evil, full of deadly poison. With it we bless the Lord and Father, and with it we curse men who were made in God's likeness! Out of the same mouth come forth blessing and cursing. These things, my brethren, ought not to be so. (James 3:3-10)

This passage offers several good pieces of advice:

➢ The inclination of our tongue is to do evil.
➢ The tongue must be tamed, but cannot be changed by man (nature).

➤ Both blessings and curses come from the tongue.

Words can bless or curse and they have power. The Bible wouldn't tell us to tame the tongue if it couldn't be done. If it can't be done by natural means, then it must be a work of the Spirit.

It is my goal every day to say this prayer: "Holy Spirit, I give you control of my tongue and my entire body. Let my words be only those that are for good and not evil." In the past I have found myself unable to utter certain words or ideas, which at the time I felt were okay but later I discovered were in error of God's word. I thank God for literally holding my tongue!

The most important thing to remember is that the words of God— the Holy Spirit-inspired words of the Bible—increase our faith.

8th Key

Increasing Faith

We must have faith and the full assurance of the authority we wield. Feed your faith by reading the word until you know what authority has been given you.

Warnings about Authority

When I first began learning about the authority we have as Christians, little was said about *limitations* to that authority. One type of authority was spoken widely about and I discovered it early in my Christian walk. The other I've only found in one teaching but knowledge of it miraculously delivered me in a time of need. There are two limits to a Christian's authority:

- ➤ Over Other People
- ➤ In Heavenly Places

In addition to these limits there are warnings the Bible gives us about how not to exercise this authority:

- ➤ Without Jesus
- ➤ Without the Gospel

There are adverse effects if either of these approaches is attempted. Before you begin exercising your authority, let us explore the fullness of our rights by talking about the limitations and warnings associated with it.

AUTHORITY OVER OTHER PEOPLE

This limitation has been mentioned, but it is worth recapping. It is logical that you do not have authority over other people. That would be taking away their God-given free will. For example, you can't effect change in the way a person raises their kids or spends their money unless they asked for your help or opinion. It is the same with our authority in the spiritual world. You cannot exercise authority over a household unless that person asks you to intervene or gives you permission to step into the situation.

That said, you are able to exert authority over spirits that are controlling people if they interfere in your family or business. What authority you have in these situations will be covered more specifically in the upcoming chapter.

IN HEAVENLY PLACES

Our lack of authority in heavenly places is a little more complicated. First, let us define what these places are.

Behold, <u>the heavens and the highest of heavens</u>
belong to the Lord your God... (Deuteronomy 10:14)

Praise the Lord! Praise the Lord from the heavens...
(Psalms 148:1)

These are two of the places in the Bible
where it refers to multiple heavens. Paul states
that there is a third heaven.

I know a man in Christ who fourteen years ago—
whether in the body I do not know, or out of the body
I do not know, [only] God knows—such a man was
caught up to the third heaven. (2 Corinthians 12:2)

If there is a third heaven, then there must
be a second and a first heaven. We have
established that this is a spiritual realm where
God lives. He has authority there, but we do
not.

The heaven, even the heavens, are the Lord's: but the
Earth hath He given to the children of men. (Psalms
115:16)

It cannot be clearer than that. God gave
Earth to man when He gave us authority over
it. Heaven is where He rules, not us.

Are there limits to man's authority on this Earth? Are there consequences if we step outside our authority? For many years I believed that "all authority" was given to me because so many big preachers were saying that. Recently, God has shown me that statement is not supported in the Word of God. When we try use authority God hasn't given us, this is wielding unauthorized authority.

The Bible says that we are "joint heirs" with Jesus (Romans 8:17) however if you look at the context, the surrounding scripture is talking about our present suffering should be endured because we are "heirs with Jesus." You inherit something and receive your inheritance when you die.

The Roman Christians were being hung on crosses and fed to lions, Paul was encouraging them of their future: When they die they would inherit eternal life in Heaven. Many times this verse is combined with being "co-laborers" with Jesus. The entire verse reads:

"For we are co-workers in God's service; you are God's field, God's building… (1 Corinthians 3:9)

We are what God uses to do His work on this Earth. A field cannot plant crops or do things on its own. God is the one directing what needs to be done, not us. We need to be sure that we are doing what God wants us to do.

Another common reference to our authority is that we have been given "all authority." Nowhere in the Bible does it say that we have been given all authority. After Jesus rose from the grave He said:

> "All authority in heaven and on earth has been given to me…" (Matthew 28:18)

If we continue reading, in the rest of that passage, the Lord tells us to go and make disciples. He never says, "I give you all authority." Jesus states clearly what authority we have been given in the Great Commission:

> Go into all the world and preach and publish openly the good news (the Gospel) to every creature [of the whole human race]... And these attesting signs will accompany those who believe:
>
> 1. In My name they will drive out demons;
> 2. They will speak in new tongues;
> 3. They will pick up serpents
> 4. If they drink anything deadly, it will not hurt them;

5. They will lay their hands on the sick, and they will be made well."

This entire list is comprised of things that are affecting men on this earth:

1. Demons reside in men
2. You speak with your physical body
3. "Pick up snakes"
4. What we ingest will not harm us - in this world
5. Healing happens to people's physical body

Every one of these is something that is afflicting us in this physical world - it is touching our physical realm. All power was given to Jesus, our Lord, and He gave us authority in these areas, not "all authority."

To further explain number three: In Strong's Concordance the Greek word "αἴρω" for "take up" can also mean to "remove from thy place." Serpents are earthly animals and often used to describe Satan and his forces as they act upon this earth. We are to remove them from their place here on Earth. How do we do that? By listening to the Holy Spirit: do we use the name of Jesus or do we need to go to the Courts of Heaven (See *Destroying Curses in the Courts of Heaven*)

There are three ways we transgress concerning authority that hasn't been given to us:

1. Taking authority over principalities, powers, and spiritual wickedness in high places.
2. Commanding the heavenly hosts or specific angels.
3. Taking authority over Leviathan.

Let's look at each one of these in detail.

Principalities, Powers, and Wickedness in High Places

Many people quote the verse, "and raised us up together, and made us sit together in the heavenly places in Christ Jesus..." (Ephesians 2:6)

It is making a huge leap to say that because we are seated with Him, that we have the same authority He has. Nowhere in the Bible does it say anything about us having ALL the authority He has. We only have what our Lord gives us, what is stated in the Bible and what

He did on this Earth. You must keep reading to find out what this verse is speaking of:

> That in the ages to come he might shew the exceeding riches of his grace in his kindness toward us through Christ Jesus. For by grace are ye saved through faith; and that not of yourselves: it is the gift of God... (Ephesians 2:7-8)

The position we hold in Christ isn't saying that we have all the authority that He has, it is saying that God's grace is being displayed in our right standing in Heaven by what Jesus did! To add to that verse and say we have all the authority He has, is very presumptuous.

If the millions of Christians on this planet could actually see what all the demons, principalities and dominions were doing in the heavens, would we really know what to do with them? If everyone had the right and began to bind and loose them, there would be total chaos. Our authority is here on the planet earth. We must remember that and stop trying to take authority over what we don't fully understand. Often people pair the previous verse with this one:

> "For we wrestle not against flesh and blood, but against principalities, against powers, against the

rulers of the darkness of this world, against spiritual wickedness in high places" (Ephesians 6:12)

Many people claim that this is proof that we occupy the same position with God as Jesus does, so we need to take authority over things in the Heavens. The chapter before this one in Ephesians, and all five verses prior to this one, talks about submitting to those in authority over us on this earth. There is nothing that speaks of us attacking anything. Quite the opposite. It says to walk in love, knowing that our battle isn't with flesh and blood. If you keep reading, the next verse gives the context:

> Therefore put on God's complete armor, that you may be able to resist and stand your ground on the evil day [of danger], and, having done all [the crisis demands], to stand [firmly in your place]. (Ephesians 6:13)

We are just supposed to stand, not to attack. After Paul describes the armor of God, he shows how to stand: by praying in the Spirit (heavenly language) and praying that our spiritual leaders are granted wisdom. That is it. Those are our instructions.

Where is there an example in the Bible of a man taking authority over things in the

Heavens? Did Jesus ever do it when He was acting as a man on this Earth. Did the disciples? The Bible says no such thing! If the disciples could have prayed and dispersed the evil powers controlling Israel, wouldn't they have done that when they were being crucified? Yet nowhere in the New Testament is there an example of them attacking principalities, pulling down strongholds in Heaven or loosing the hosts of Heaven to come and battle on their behalf.

Here is a New Testament verse warning us about taking actions other than this:

> Nevertheless in like manner, these dreamers also corrupt the body, scorn and reject authority and government, and revile and libel and scoff at [heavenly] glories (the glorious ones).

> But when [even] the archangel Michael, contending with the devil, judicially argued (disputed) about the body of Moses, he dared not [presume to] bring an abusive condemnation against him, but [simply] said, The Lord rebuke you! (Jude 1:8-9)

The word translated "glories" in the Amplified and "dignitaries" in the King James Bible is the Greek word, *doxa* which can mean "of the angels." We know this is the right translation because it goes on to give an example of Michael not condemning Satan but instead asking the Lord to do so. This is an example of how we are to act and it is after Jesus had risen. He has been given all power, we have not.

Jesus clearly gave us power to cast out demons. If we are "casting out" it must be "in" someone. Some are claiming we can move against principalities because the "legion" of demons inside the man which Jesus cast out into the pigs (Matthew 8) would constitute a principality because it was a military unit. We need to stick to the facts stated in the Bible instead of presuming:

➢ The Legion was in a man - we have authority to cast out what is inside someone
➢ "Principalities, powers and spiritual wickedness in High Places" - the High Places are in the heavens, so principalities are in the heavens.

We cannot mix the two things together. If the spirit is affecting:

➢ an area - neighborhood
➢ a business, or school

> ➤ a city
> ➤ a country

We do not own these and do not have authority over these things. Geographical areas are under the rule of a principality operating in the heavens and it is not ours to control. Unfortunately, people are still commanding things in Heaven:

➤ Individuals reading prayers from books or saying "amen" to prayers online, on television or in church.
➤ in group prayer meetings
➤ in prayer marches around cities

Some examples of what they are wrongly commanding are:

1. spirit of abortion
2. spirit of violence
3. spirit of adultery
4. spirit of witchcraft

What if you see these things? A woman, let's call her Tammy, was shown a dragon over her daughters school and insisted that this was revealed so she could cast it down. Since there is no example of someone on Earth casting down a principality, that is a direction that the Bible does not support. Tammy was also given a vision as she was praying over a nation:

> "I suddenly had a vision of myself in the heavenlies looking down on the earth with this demonic principality. As I prayed in the spirit, I saw angels being dispatched from heaven. While continuing to pray over this situation I saw the Lord several steps behind me..."

The Holy Spirit was trying to show her the right way to handle the situation according to the Word of God. If a principality over an area is revealed, pray as the Bible tells us to, in the Heavenly language. When we yield our tongue to the Holy Spirit, we are not praying, God is speaking. What we say is authorized by God because the Holy Spirit is the one speaking: God is speaking through our mouth!

Unfortunately, Tammy believed that God was telling her that she had all authority, that she had been given special authority over principalities. We can hear from God and we can hear from the enemy who loves to imitate God. We must ALWAYS test what we hear by comparing it to the Word of God. If you don't find it in His word, then it isn't from Him. Was there ever anyone in the Bible, even Jesus Himself, that took authority over principalities? Then it is a bit prideful to think you have more authority than He did.

What about the verse that says those that believe "will do even greater things than these," (John 14:12). Couldn't that refer to tearing down strongholds and principalities in the Heavens?

Absolutely not. God is always the same. He will never contradict what He has already said. The Earth is man's, the Heavens are the Lord's. Pray in the Spirit, let God say what He wants done through your mouth. This is what the Bible says about Principalities.

Leviathan

Leviathan is not a single demon. The Bible labels the armies of Egypt as Leviathan. Satan's network in the spirit realm, hovering over the Earth, called by the same name in that realm. There are 7 heads or strong leaders who are his generals controlling his army - they have different categories of abilities. (Revelation 12:3)

When we say an attack of "Leviathan" we are saying that it is a coordinated attack by the armies of Satan. The Bible tells us there is only one who can deal with this: The Lord is the one who can battle Leviathan.

> In that day the Lord will punish Leviathan the fleeing serpent... (Isaiah 27:1)

The 41st chapter of Job tells us the most about this army.

> Can you fill his skin with harpoons, Or his head with fishing spears? Lay your hand on him; Remember the battle [with him]; you will not do such [an ill-advised thing] again! Behold, his [assailant's] hope and expectation [of defeating Leviathan] is false; Will not one be overwhelmed even at the sight of him? No one is so fierce [and foolhardy] that he dares to stir up Leviathan; Who then is he who can stand before Me [or dares to contend with Me, the beast's creator]? (Job 41: 7-10)

If you sense a multi-pronged attack upon your life, cry out to your Lord who can free you! Do not try to attack Leviathan who is the army of Satan in the Heavens.

Commanding Angels

There is a very popular wrong teaching out that we can "command our angels" to do things. I believed this for many years. However when someone asked me what verse I was standing on, I searched many books by well-known ministers to see where their Biblical support was. This was all I found:

"Are they not all ministering spirits, sent forth to minister for them who shall be heirs of salvation?" (Hebrews 1:14 KJV)

When we examine this in the Amplified version which goes back to the original text to give a fuller meaning, this is what we find:

"Are not the angels all ministering spirits (servants) sent out in the service [of God for the assistance] of those who are to inherit salvation?"

This makes it clear that our angels are in God's service to help us. They are not our servants to command.

Heavenly Hosts:

There is a certain female minister who has been declaring that we can release or command the heavenly host to tear down strongholds. She quotes this verse:

> Bless the Lord, you His angels, who excel in strength, who do His word, heeding the voice of His word. (Psalm 103:20)

However if you listen carefully to her video on this topic, she has changed it to say, "The angels hearken to YOUR words." This is not what the Bible states. "His" is capitalized, so it is referring to God. It is clear that the heavenly host heed God's words not mans!

When Jesus was being arrested He said,

> "Do you suppose that I cannot appeal to My Father, and He will immediately provide Me with more than twelve legions [more than 80,000] of angels?" (Matthew 26:53 AMP)

If our Lord had to ask His Father and wasn't commanding the angels, what makes us think we can command instead of ask? The Bible also tells us that the angels are God's servants and the ones assigned to the "little ones" have their face turned toward God. Angels are commanded by God the Father, not us.

In the first visit in the Courts of Heaven where we address these issues, many people are instantly healed, some wake up the next morning healed of things we had no idea they were suffering with. Clearing the charges is as easy as saying, "I am sorry, God, that I took authority in the Heavens that wasn't mine. I know now that my authority is with things on the Earth and I won't take authority in the heavens again. I plead the blood over these things and ask that all cases against me for these things are dismissed in Jesus' name."

Consequences of Unauthorized Authority

If you love Me, you will keep My commandments. And I will ask the Father, and He will give you another Advocate to be with you forever— (John 14:15)

For those who are led by the Spirit of God are the children of God. (Romans 8:14)

These two verses should always be foremost in our thoughts. How do we know that we belong to Jesus and that we love Him? We keep His commandments: to love one another and to love God. By doing this or our willingness to start doing this, we receive the Holy Spirit.

We know we are loving one another when we have evidence of the Holy Spirit being in our lives. This is known as having the "fruit of the Spirit:" love, joy, peace, forbearance, kindness, goodness, faithfulness, gentleness and self-control. If you are struggling with these things, the Courts of Heaven may help set you free of the enemies influence so that you can begin growing in these things.

Now that you know what it looks like to have the Holy Spirit in charge of your life, we must always remember that "those who are led by the Spirit are the children of God." Yes, Jesus gave us His name, but did the Holy Spirit tell you to use it? We must be led by the Spirit in order to be operating as in our authority as a child of God.

There is a danger in trying to take authority that isn't ours. God is fair and just. When we attack the enemy illegally, he gets to attack us back - illegally.

In the fall of 2016, the Holy Spirit urged me to take up my duties to intercede for my nation's leaders. I did this in the courts of

Heaven, as He urged, then I took the next logical step: I took authority over all those spiritual rulers in high places. After all, the Bible says:

> For our wrestling is not against flesh and blood, but against the principalities, against the powers, against the world-rulers of this darkness, against the <u>spiritual hosts of wickedness in the heavenly places.</u> (Ephesians 6:12 ESV)

I knew that the spiritual king of Tyre had impeded God's messenger, so I figured I would take them out of commission in order that they wouldn't hinder God's plan. It seemed the logical thing to do.

A couple of months later, God sent me across the country on a three-and-a-half-week mission. The moment I stepped off the plane, my throat began to ache. For the first twelve days I was plagued by a sore throat and fever that wouldn't go away.

Usually when sickness comes upon me, I spend a few hours in prayer, worship, and meditation of God's word and my symptoms go away. By day eleven I had enough. I curled up in my bed and put on Christian TV programs to bolster my faith.

My fever spiked. Nausea and dizziness overcame me each time I stood up. "What is going on?" I thought. "I've researched the word, I know my authority; this sickness is trespassing!"

I lay in bed, feeling like I could lose consciousness at any moment. I refused to give up. I knew something was wrong and I needed to fix it. The next show I played on the DVR was talking about the authority of God. It quoted the verse about the Heavens being the Lords. Then the host, let's call him John, talked about a time when three pastors called him about things that were going on in their church:

- Five women had miscarried in the same month last year; four other pregnant women were spotting blood and would soon miscarry in that same month.
- Two pastors either had a child that had run away or one who went missing.

While seeking an answer John was sent a dream with the previously stated verses. When he called the pastors back, sure enough, each one had been leading their congregation against the spiritual powers influencing their region. Once the pastors repented for trespassing on God's authority, the situations resolved within 24 hours:

➢ All four women stopped spotting and had full-term pregnancies.
➢ Both missing children called their parents and returned home.

After pulling up the Bible app on my phone and reading the entire chapters that were quoted, I realized I had violated the structure of authority that God had put in place. Since I had illegally attacked the enemy, he now had the legal right to attack *me*. Of course Satan waited until I was away from my home base and working for God to retaliate.

I didn't waste any time. "Mighty God, I am so sorry I overstepped my authority and came against the enemy in the heavens. I won't ever do that again! I plead the blood of Jesus over this sin and I thank you that it is blotted out of all records in Heaven. Father, I thank you that the enemy has no more legal right to assault me."

The quiet knowing in my spirit came. I knew that by morning I would see the attack broken and be restored to health by the end of the next day. It came to pass exactly as the

Holy Spirit brought it to me. I went from having a high fever and barely able to stand, to being completely healed in 24 hours.

This was a lesson I likely won't ever forget. I will never again try to take authority over spiritual rulers in heavenly places. Search the scriptures and see if there is even one example of a human being attacking things in the spiritual realm. I looked and found nothing. If I don't see it in the Bible, I don't presume to think I can do it.

** Added note: After taking hundreds of people to the Courts of Heaven, we have discovered these actions result in extra "bogus" charges. See "Destroying Curses in the Courts of Heaven" for more details.

9th Key
Knowing the Limitations

Beware of overstepping your authority: The Heavens are the Lord's, but the Earth He has given to men. Use your authority on Earth and our physical realm only, to attack principalities.

Benefits of Authority

Now that we know what authority is and how to get it, how can we use it? That is a loaded question. There are many benefits to being a Christian, but this book is dedicated to the basics of authority. Let's focus on the main scripture where Jesus commands us to use His authority:

> These signs will accompany those who have believed: <u>in My name they will cast out demons</u>, they will speak in new tongues; they will pick up serpents, and if they drink anything deadly, it will not hurt them; they will lay hands on the sick, and they will get well. (Mark 16:17-18)

These are his instructions for ALL who believe who are follow Jesus' prior commandment:

> And he said unto them, Go ye into all the world, and preach the gospel to every creature... (Mark 16:15 KJV)

This commandment is taking place out in the world where people are hearing about the

Gospel, about Jesus, for the first time! Let's continue reading:

> He who has believed [in Me] and has been baptized will be saved [from the penalty of God's wrath and judgment]; but he who has not believed will be condemned. These signs will accompany those who have believed..." (Mark 16:16-17)

Remember, one of the meanings of "baptized" is to let go of your old self and become a new creation in God or to be born again. The act of being dunked in water is just a physical ceremony to demonstrate what has transpired in our spirits. We are overwhelmed by the Holy Spirit (often depicted as water).

When we speak about what Jesus has done, the Holy Spirit comes in power and gives us a particular kind of authority at that moment. It is not over other people, but over specific things. Let us examine each of these items so that we are sure of the basic authority God has given us.

ATTACKS OF THE ENEMY

Jesus begins His instructions by saying, "in My name they will cast out demons." The name of the king represents the authority of that king. With these words, Jesus is handing authority over demons to anyone who believes that He is the Son of God and has taken Him as their Lord after hearing the Gospel for the first time.

The Greek word used for demons is *daimonion,* which means a spirit that is lower than God but more powerful than man. Jesus wanted His disciples to know that when the power of the Holy Spirit was present and the Gospel was being preached, the person that believed cold have spirits removed from them, even those more powerful than they are. Going back to the policeman analogy, an officer of a smaller build can still subdue a larger person through the authority given to him by society.

The next thing that is mentioned is "speak with new tongues." To really know what is being said here we need to look at the second place in the Word of God where this scene is recounted from another perspective.

The disciples were pestering Jesus about when He would establish His earthly kingdom. After He told them it was for God to know, He redirected their attention to what they needed to focus on:

<u>But you will receive power and ability when the Holy Spirit comes upon you</u>; and you will be My witnesses [to tell people about Me] both in Jerusalem and in all Judea, and Samaria, and even to the ends of the Earth. (Acts 1:8)

Like most eyewitness accounts this is about what Jesus was giving them, just coming from a different perspective. How do we know this? Because in the next verse it says Jesus ascended into Heaven. It was happening at the same time as the end of the chapter in Mark. This is referring back to the second thing Jesus said, "You will speak in new tongues." The Greek word used for new is *kainos,* which also means unknown or unseen until now.

The disciples had to go to Jerusalem and wait until they received the power of the Holy Spirit. The sign of this power would be speaking in an unknown tongue. When this power came upon them in the upper room they spilled out into the street and began babbling in unknown languages. (Acts 1:12-20)

The statements following how one would "speak in new tongues" occur after the power of the Holy Spirit comes upon you. We will leave the remainder of that verse for another book about the power and gifts of the Holy Spirit. Now we will focus on what authority we have over the enemy. There are also a surprising number of health issues where the root cause is a demonic attack. They include:

1. Demonized individuals (demonically controlling people)
2. Curses affecting:
3. Mental health
4. Wellness
5. Financial Prosperity

Demonized People

Satan and his minions are crafty; they have been manipulating people for thousands of years. Their influence can be subtle and can creep into anyone's life, even a Christian's. If you are involved with spirits of any kind, through a Ouija board, séances, spirit writing, ones that appear in plain sight and begin speaking to you, or any other spirit being, God gives us a way to test them and see if they are for man or against mankind and God.

Beloved, do not believe every spirit, but test the spirits to see whether they are from God, because many false prophets have gone out into the world. By this you know the Spirit of God: <u>every spirit that confesses that Jesus Christ has come in the flesh is</u>

<u>from God</u>; and every spirit that does not confess Jesus is not from God. (1 John 4:1-3)

To find out if a spirit is from God, simply ask, "Do you confess that Jesus Christ has come in the flesh." Demonic spirits won't say yes, they will flee. There are three stages of influence demons can have upon a person.

1. Depression
2. Oppression
3. Possession

In a battle, recognizing the tactics and strategies of your enemy is the first step toward victory. If you refuse to admit you are under attack, you will never be victorious in battle. To enforce your authority you need to know when the enemy is crossing the line.

Depression

The root word of depression is "depress," which means to reduce the strength or activity of. This suffix "ion" denotes or indicates condition. Combine the root and suffix and you get the condition of being reduced in strength or activity. This is the most subtle and common form of attack from the demonic realm. If our adversary can reduce our activity, and deplete our strength, then we are not taking as much ground for the Kingdom of God.

Just as the more conventional meaning of depression suggests, this is a mental attack. It can be as subtle as demons assigned to putting thoughts into your head.

> …we are taking every thought and purpose captive to the obedience of Christ… (2 Corinthians 10:5)

Inherently, we have a sinful nature so there are some thoughts that come out of our sinful nature. Then there are thoughts that are attacks of the enemy. The Bible tells us we each have an angel guarding us. Satan is an imitator of God but he is neither omniscient nor omnipresent. He doesn't know everything nor, as previously stated, can he be in more than one place at a time.

The old concept of a devil on one shoulder and an angel on the other isn't far from the truth. Satan assigns demons to each person. Their sole job is to follow you around and prevent you from reaching your full potential. These low-level imps don't have much power other than interjecting thoughts to try and get you to veer off your path, thus giving them more power.

In this situation, you might ask, well, how can a person control their thoughts? German theologian Martin Luther said, "You cannot keep birds from flying over your head, but you can keep them from building a nest in your hair." This is a perfect example of what happens if we don't take authority over negative thoughts. When these sinful, destructive thoughts are acknowledged and accepted (by speaking them out loud or acting upon them) then the demon assigned to us gains ground. Remember, whatever you obey you give authority to. If you give into these thoughts, by dwelling upon them or acting upon them, the spirit who initiated them worms its way deeper into your life. Eventually it can lead to oppression.

Oppression

If you relinquish ground to the enemy, this can lead to oppression. The definition of oppression is continued unjust or cruel treatment or control. This is where demonic assaults begin affecting your body. Many people who have a gift of seeing into the spirit realm have described what they refer to as black masses attached to people's bodies not unlike a fungus or growth. These demons are similar to leeches, and if you let them attach themselves to you they will feed on the authority you give them, exerting more and more control.

Oppression can manifest itself by showing up in the physical world, and in more ways than I can list here. The Bible doesn't record each and every way, but it does say this:

> …how God anointed Jesus of Nazareth with the Holy Spirit and with great power; and He went around doing good and healing all who were oppressed by the devil, because God was with Him. (Acts 10:38)

This clearly shows that a result of oppression is physical conditions that need healing because healing occurred when the oppression was broken. It also shows that Satan can be a cause of a physical sickness.

Recent studies about the way our brain works shows that when you think about things repetitively it forms physical neural pathways that are easily accessed. The more you think about a thing, the easier it is to access. This is why the Bible commands us in the following ways:

Do not conform to the pattern of this world, but be transformed by the renewing of your mind. (Romans 12:2 NIV)

Putting the right word in your heart and mind can lead to a transformation. The word also encourages us to focus on good things:

Finally, believers, whatever is true, whatever is honorable and worthy of respect, whatever is right and confirmed by God's word, whatever is pure and wholesome, whatever is lovely and brings peace, whatever is admirable and of good repute; if there is any excellence, if there is anything worthy of praise, think continually on these things [center your mind on them, and implant them in your heart]. (Philippians 4:7-8)

Before man knew that pigs carried parasites and diseases that could be transmitted to man, the Bible called them unclean and told us not to eat them. Before we knew about heavy metals in shrimp and eel, God told His people not to eat them. Now, top neurologists have found that repetitive thinking establishes pathways in the brain. Negative thoughts develop caustic pathways that release cancer-causing, destructive material into our systems. Research shows that 87% of all diseases are connected to the release of toxins in the brain. (Source: Dr. Caroline Leaf, PhD in Communication Pathology specializing in Neuropsychology, University of Cape Town, South Africa)

Repetitive negative thought patterns are highways allowing spiritual oppression. Christians are not immune to this type of attack from the enemy. Through Jesus, this is what the authority we have been given should be used for.

Possession

> When He arrived at the other side in the country of the Gadarenes, two demon-possessed men coming out of the tombs met Him. (Matthew 8:28)

The Greek word *daimonizomai* is translated "possessed" in some versions of the Bible and demonized in others. To be demonized means to be under the control or influence of evil spirits. When you possess something, you own it. If a person is possessed, a demon will take full control over them, thus the root of this terminology. Survivors of possession have described it as being able to see, but unable to

control so much as the blinking of their eyes.
Possession can only occur in two ways:

1. Invitation
2. Rape

Playing with Ouija Boards, séances, and
spirit guides all involve spirits that do not come
from God. If they are not with God, rather they
are aligned with Satan. They will lie and
manipulate to gain influence with you. These
spirits can appear in familiar forms of loved
ones with information they have gained from
watching us our entire lives. Their goal is to get
us to invite them into us so that they have a
home. You can invite the Holy Spirit to come
inside you and He will advise and help you or
you can invite a demon inside who will attempt
to trick and manipulate you.

The only way for a spirit to enter a person
without their permission is through rape. I
believe it is because our spirit is damaged
during the attack, which allows for a transfer of
a spirit. The Bible tells us that when a man and
woman have sex they become "one flesh"
(Matthew 10:8). In biblical times, many gods
were worshiped with sexual acts. For example,
in the story of Balaam, a soothsayer advised
the king of Moab that the only way to defeat
God's people was to have them betray God so

He would take His hand (protection and favor) off them. Priestesses were sent to the camp and many of the Israelites engaged with them in sexual acts of worship to another god. Though it is not specifically stated, there seems to be something of spiritual significance that occurs during sex. This is why we are supposed to wait until we commit to a lifetime relationship (marriage) with someone before we engage in intercourse. Perhaps a sexual act, in some way, affects our spirit. This would explain why rape is the only way a demon can possess a person without an invitation.

This hypothesis also explains why I have seen children who were conceived through rape who are also possessed through no fault of their own. The children were not old enough to invite a demon inside; the only common ground was their conception through rape.

Regardless of how a spirit comes to be in a position of authority and take complete control over a person, one fact remains: God has provided a way for everyone to be set free. If a spirit has taken up residence in your spirit, it can be cast out through the authority of Jesus, though it may take a visit to the Courts of Heaven which we will discuss in the next book.

How to Use Authority

Listen to the voice of the Holy Spirit so you can enforce your authority, starting with the areas under your control–your home and your family. What if your spouse isn't on board with the concept of enforcing your authority or isn't even a Christian? Even worse, what if they are actively participating with spiritual practices that are not of God? Can you still protect your home and your family or should you consider leaving your spouse?

> If any [believing] brother has a wife who does not believe [in Christ], and she consents to live with him, <u>he must not leave her</u>. And if any [believing] woman has an unbelieving husband, and he consents to live with her, she must not leave him… (1 Corinthians 7:12-13)

The next several verses go on to explain that your children are holy because of your relationship with God and that your spouse may be saved because of your walk with God. If your faith is strong enough, you should not leave your spouse unless you are in physical danger or they have been unfaithful.

The first step to declaring your authority is to dedicate your possession for use in God's kingdom by anointing it.

ANOINTING WITH OIL

God gave His chosen people instructions to consecrate not only the tent which held His presence, but all the instruments in it. This kept Satan from touching or interfering with things that were dedicated to God. Consecration was done by smearing the recipient with an "anointing oil" created by combining particular ingredients. According to the Talmud (the complete book of Jewish ceremonial and civil law), the anointing oil was made only once in Jewish history, by Moses (Exodus 30:31–33). It proved to be enough for the whole period—from the anointing of Aaron and his sons until the remainder was hidden away by Josiah.

Since then, God's people have used regular oil poured from a horn of a priest. This was done for many reasons and typically a dedication was pronounced over it, declaring it to be God's.

You shall make of these a holy anointing oil, a
perfume mixture, the work of a perfumer; it shall be a
sacred anointing oil. You shall anoint the Tent of
Meeting with it, and the ark of the Testimony, and
the table [for the bread] and all its utensils, and the
lampstand... (Exodus 30:25-27)

The word anoint is *mashach,* meaning to
smear. This word was used to describe oil that
was smeared on the head of sheep to keep
insects out of their ears. As the Israelites
smeared the items in the temple for use, God
placed them within His protection.

Oil, in general, was one of the symbols of
the Holy Spirit. Now that we are aware of the
power of spoken words, we know that the
prayers empowered the ceremonies. While
using the oil with an act of smearing was a step
of faith God required in order to activate the
anointing in the physical realm.

The Old Testament is a shadow of what
Jesus fulfills. When we take Jesus as Lord one
of the benefits is the gift of the Holy Spirit. (See
"Why Doesn't God Speak to Me?" for more
information on this.) He is the oil and we are
anointed because He resides in us. This makes
each of us a temple of God.

Do you not know that your body is a temple of the Holy Spirit who is within you, whom you have [received as a gift] from God, and that you are not your own [property]? (1 Corinthians 6:17)

As a temple of God, we are anointed when the Holy Spirit comes to reside in us, but our homes are not. However, we can declare objects for God's use by anointing them with oil and saying a quick prayer of dedication over them.

Why We Anoint Things

Spiritual beings can see our physical world. They know what is occurring and can affect people's objects to varying degrees. Anointing objects with blessed oil declares them for the Kingdom of God to the spiritual realm. I like to think of them as glowing with the power of the Holy Spirit after they are dedicated. By doing this, spiritual beings will know that the person inside the home or vehicle is aware of their authority through Jesus and may think twice before trying something.

Soon after I rededicated my life to the Lord, I received the gift of discernment from the Holy Spirit. As a result, I began to see demons. I would cast them out and they would come back in a few days.

I grew tired of having to do this and sought an answer. Once the authority of anointing things with blessed oil was explained to me I anointed every window and outside door of my house. Demons stopped popping in after that. (The full story appears in "Angels Believe in You.") Anointing your house with blessed oil should be one of the first things a believer does when they understand the principles behind it. How do you get oil that is blessed to use for anointing?

Creating Blessed Oil

Another perk of being a Christian is that Jesus is our High Priest.

This hope [this confident assurance] we have as an anchor of the soul… a safe and steadfast hope that enters within the veil [of the heavenly temple, that most Holy Place in which the very presence of God dwells], where Jesus has entered [in advance] as a forerunner for us, having become a High Priest forever according to the order of Melchizedek. (Hebrews 6:19-20)

The High Priest is the one who pronounces the blessing over the oil so that it is "anointed." Remember, our spirits have access to Heaven right now—we are seated with Jesus and we have direct access to God.

> For it is through Him that we both have a [direct] way of approach in one Spirit to the Father. (Ephesians 2:18)

Jesus is seated at the right hand of God. He is our High Priest. We have direct access to Him. He is the one who blesses the oil; all we have to do is ask. A simple prayer, said in faith, knowing that He will do what we ask, is all it takes to have your own blessed oil to use for anointing. While you hold a container of oil in your hand say a prayer like this:

> Dear Jesus,
> I come before You, my High Priest. I ask that you bless this oil so that it is suitable to anoint things, which are dedicated for your use. I ask this in Your name, Amen.

Jesus is ready and willing to act as our High Priest. Things we use and places we stay can be dedicated to God with this oil now that it is blessed and ready to use.

Anointing Objects

Now that you have blessed oil, who is it that may actually use it? Priests were the ones who dedicated the objects in the temple to God with the anointed oil. The Bible tells us that those who are believers are priests.

> You [believers], like living stones, are being built up into a spiritual house for a holy and dedicated priesthood, to offer spiritual sacrifices [that are] acceptable and pleasing to God through Jesus Christ. (1 Peter 2:5)

> But you are a chosen race, a royal priesthood, a consecrated nation, a [special] people for God's own possession, so that you may proclaim the excellences [the wonderful deeds and virtues and perfections] of Him who called you out of darkness into His marvelous light. (1 Peter 2:9)

When you take Jesus as Lord, you become a priest in the eyes of God. As a priest you can dedicate your home, your vehicle, and any other object you own to God and use for God's kingdom.

I knew a woman who was trying to post something online that she really believed God

114

told her to do. Her computer kept dying and shutting down. She prayed over some oil and dedicated that computer to God and told the enemy to take his hands off God's property. She never had an issue with her computer again.

Dedicating an item to God with blessed oil is simple.

1. Dip your finger in the oil.
2. Declare, "In Jesus' name I dedicate this _____ to God for use in His work." (Fill in the blank using words such as home, car, computer, etc....)
3. Smear the oil on the object: window or door seal or any part of an object.

Just like that, you have declared to the spirit realm that this property belongs to God, and that you are aware of the authority given to you by the death and resurrection of Jesus.

Anointed Oil for Healing

There is a debate in the body of Christ as to whether or not it is necessary to anoint people with oil when praying for healing or casting out demons. The need for using oil is centered largely on two verses of scripture.

> Is anyone among you sick? He should call in the church elders (the spiritual guides). And they should pray over him, anointing him with oil in the Lord's name. (James 5:14)

If you don't read the next verse, it would seem that the oil is a key ingredient in the healing. However, the next verse says, "It is the prayer of faith that will save him who is sick." this makes it clear that the prayer is what brings healing. A second verse is used to debate the requirement of oil for healing the sick:

> And they were casting out many demons and were anointing with oil many who were sick, and healing them. (Mark 6:13)

This verse is referring to the time when Jesus sent the disciples to cast out demons and heal the sick in His name. Jesus never instructed them to use oil, only His name. So why did they anoint with oil?

The Bible speaks of many uses for oil other than the dedication of sacred object and blessing. It was used to honor men and God

(Judges 9:9), a symbol of joy (Psalms 45:8), and favor or status (Deuteronomy 33:24, Psalms 23:5). Therefore, oil was to be withheld from offerings associated with disgrace, sorrow, and disfavor, just as it was withheld from the body in a time of mourning (II Samuel 12:20, Daniel 10:3). During this biblical time, oil was also used to make perfume, and so the expression "anoint oneself" took on a different meaning. This explains why people didn't perfume themselves during a period of mourning. It is akin to the custom of honoring the deceased by not wearing brightly colored garments to their funeral.

A compelling discussion that the use of oil is based in tradition rather than essential in healing prayers can be found in Leviticus Chapters 13 and 14. In these chapters the treatment of lepers is discussed. If a leper was found to be clean, oil was placed on his right ear, right hand, and the big toe of his right foot on the eighth day. This was not blessed oil, just normal oil. Rather it symbolized that the man was once again in good standing before God and now able to:

1. Walk with God (toe)
2. Hear from God (ear)
3. Work for God (hand)

The oil was placed upon the person as a symbol that they had been cleansed and healed. It was a tradition that signified their right standing with God and their ability to receive blessings from Him.

The instructions of our Lord should be the final word for us in every matter. There is not a single mention of oil being necessary when Jesus prayed for people. Neither did He tell His disciples to bring oil with them so that people could be healed. Therefore, it isn't a necessary ingredient, only a symbolic tradition.

As with most things, Satan mimics God. In the ancient world it became common practice to anoint oneself with oil for various reasons including as a means to show one's dedication to gods.

> As oil penetrates your flesh, so may they [the gods] make this curse enter into your flesh. (D.J. Wiseman, The Vassal-Treaties of Esarhaddon, 1958)

Be assured, this was God's way first. Everything else is a mere imitation of the perfect plan of God.

Authority Issues

What if a demon doesn't leave when you use the name of Jesus? There could be many causes. Even the disciples had an issue with a demon and the father had to go directly to Jesus. Let us keep this to three basic things that can have an effect on the spiritual realm (others will be addressed in Book 3 of the *Believers Boot Camp* series by Lynn Hardy):

1. Our Surety
2. Other's Rights
3. Prayer and Fasting

Our Surety

You must know that you have authority. You must know from whom you have been given authority. Do you know the authority in the Name that is above every name? Have you heard from the Holy Spirit? There is no shame in acknowledging when you are on a learning curve.

Other's Rights

If you are having dealings with someone and the Holy Spirit brings you discernment that it is a demonic influence, you can bind the spirit from interfering. However, you may not be able to cast a demon out of someone who has not given you authority to do so.

Some examples of times when demons were cast out without permission include:

1. Paul: when a slave woman who functioned as a fortune-teller was following them. (Acts 16:16-18)
2. Jesus: who cast a legion out of a demon-possessed man in the tombs. (Mark 5)

This could have been done for one of two reasons. First, each of these had a desire to be free of the spirit because both were grateful after it happened. Perhaps the level of authority and communication with God was so high that permission wasn't needed. Could it be that God revealed the desire of the person to be free directly to the disciples?

Secondly, it could have been that the demons were attempting to interfere in their mission for God. We do have authority over demons that come into contact with our realm of influence, including our ministry work.

Regardless of the reason, if you listen to the Holy Spirit, He will not lead you astray. He will enable and facilitate what He tells you to do. Focus on your connection to the Holy Spirit, asking Him to speak more clearly to you.

Prayer and Fasting

Perhaps the most controversial pair of passages about exercising authority over demons comes from these two separate accounts of an incident, one which appears in Mark and another in Matthew. There was a young boy possessed by a demon. The disciples couldn't banish it, so the father brought his son to Jesus who said:

> O unbelieving (faithless) generation, how long shall I be with you? How long shall I put up with you? Bring him to Me! (Mark 9:19)

After the Lord cast the demon out, His followers asked:

> Why could not we cast it out? And He saith unto them, Because of your little faith: for verily I say unto you, if ye have faith as a grain of mustard seed,

ye shall say unto this mountain, remove hence to yonder place; and it shall remove; and nothing shall be impossible unto you. *But this kind goeth not out save by prayer and fasting.* (Matthew 17:19-21)

Jesus answers why they couldn't cast it out: lack of faith. The last part of the quote is italicized; it was added to the original text when translators inferred this based on other references in the Bible. Mark's accounts have "prayer and fasting" as the reason the demon didn't come out.

However, many think that prayer and fasting is *not* something we do to move God to do something. Rather, uttering the name of His beloved Son, Jesus is enough. The question is, could we add anything of value to that? It would be like saying, Jesus, you suffered and died, but let me give up food, and then Your name is good enough.

The point of the fast is to spend more time focused on God. When we deny ourselves basic necessities such as eating, we put God above our physical needs and desires. Depending on God in this way will increase our faith in His ability to overcome all obstacles.

There are many types of fasting. Partial fasting is when you abstain from certain things or one where you only consume water. A complete fast can be very dangerous and one should never fast unless it is in response to the urgings of the Holy Spirit. Let Him guide you to know what you should fast from and for how long it should continue.

Prayer is a communion with the Heavenly Father and the Lord, which also increases our faith. It is clear from considering both the accounts of Mark and Matthew that faith can be increased by prayer and fasting. Your faith can affect your authority.

Advanced Authority

Up until now we have been discussing basic authority: authority every believer has been given. This is for every member of the body of Christ—the worldwide church.

It is God's will for us to seek Him and discover the destiny He has planned for us since the beginning of time. He created us specifically for this destiny. This destiny is revealed in a vision. The Bible shows us this:

> "And it shall be in the last days," God says, "That I will pour forth of My Spirit on all mankind; and your <u>sons and your daughters</u> shall prophesy, and your <u>young men</u> shall see visions, and your <u>old men</u> shall dream dreams…" (Acts 2:17 NASB)

The ages of the people in this verse are not referring to a physical age; it is spiritual. "Sons and daughters" calls attention to when you first come to God and spiritually you are still just a child. "Young men" this is when you have learned enough about God to dedicate your life to Him. Then you will get visions of God's ultimate destiny. The visions he refers to are 20/20; they are not metaphorical. They are straightforward and clear in order that there is no mistaking what God is calling you to do. Once you accept this and continue feeding your spirit on the word of God, learning more about his ways, you become an "old man." This is not only for the male gender. This is referring to all mankind. He is speaking about the elders of the church—those who have grown and developed in the ways of God.

It is up to us to accept our destiny and begin seeking Him so we can walk toward that destiny. This is a time of testing and training. (More about this will be discussed in a future book.) For now, let us address the fullness of what Jesus said:

> And Jesus came up and spoke to them, saying, "<u>All authority has been given to Me</u> in Heaven and on Earth. Go therefore and make disciples of all the nations, baptizing them in the name of the Father and the Son and the Holy Spirit, teaching them to observe all that I commanded you; and lo, I am with you always, even to the end of the age." (Matthew 28:18 NASB)

He said, "All authority has been given to HIM." He did not say "I give *all authority to you*." Jesus told his disciples to go and He would be with them. The holder of all authority in Heaven and Earth will be beside you when you listen to what He says and go where He tells you to go.

In plain English, He is saying, "Look, all authority is mine and I got your back. Just go where I tell you to go and do what I tell you to do and I'll be there to give you what you need."

Once you accept the destiny God has for you, all the authority you need to accomplish that destiny will be available as Jesus walks beside you. You need to get good at hearing His voice so you know what to say, and recognize what authority it is appropriate to use at the moment it is needed. That is what *Believers' Boot Camp* is about—the ability to get good at hearing and doing what He says.

Think of it like this. The Secret Service protects the President of the United States and other dignitaries. They can walk into a police station and take control over local jurisdictions and their authority because of their position of closeness and connection to the President, the leader of this nation. Should the President ever be in danger, their authority is elevated to a new level.

In addition to this degree of immense power and access, they are authorized to do whatever is necessary to protect the President when he is beside them. They can take possession of someone's property or even take the life of a person who threatens the safety and security of the Commander in Chief. Similarly, the closer we walk to Jesus the more His authority flows through us.

A woman in my church, Alice, once demonstrated a perfect example of this. She lives on the edge of Boise, Idaho. One summer a fire started in its foothills close by. She could see it from a window in her house.

As smoke billowed in, Alice began praying in her heavenly language. Words came to her mind and she spoke them out. "Wind, in Jesus' name, I command you to turn and blow away from these houses." Next, she spoke to the fire, "In Jesus' name I command you fire to die down." She continued to pray as she had been guided to do by the Holy Spirit.

The following morning, the *Idaho Statesman* announced: "A sudden wind shift pushed the fire back from the homes and then calmer winds prevailed, giving fire crews the window they needed to gain control of the fire... The winds did prove to be advantageous for firefighters by moving from one direction to another... The winds changed course and then calmed down, halting the fire's spread."[ii]

Alice had commanded the wind and it had obeyed her and so did the fire. Does this mean that she should run headlong into every forest fire and command the wind and fire? No. Jesus gave her the authority she needed at that moment. If she winds up in the path of another fire during her walk with Him, I am sure He will, once again, give her the authority needed.

10th Key
Advance Authority

Learn to hear from and walk with the Lord. ALL authority has been given to Him. He will give you what you need to get the job done!

Final Words

God made a particularly strong impression on me in 2016. He told me to add two elements to all free books:

First Word

Freely you have received; freely give. (Matthew 10:8 NIV)

Most people only apply this verse to what is mentioned directly before it.

Heal the sick, raise the dead, and cleanse those who have leprosy, drive out demons. (Matthew 10:7)

This is the inspired word of God. There is purpose in every nuance of what is said. In this case, we must also examine what is not being said: it doesn't say, "Freely heal, freely raise the dead, freely cleanse, freely cast out." This would have clearly defined what we should do freely.

Instead we have Jesus giving instruction and direction. First He reveals what He has called them to do and empowers those whom

He has set on a task. Then, He adds the parameters, "you did nothing to earn this power or knowledge; I give it freely to you. You do the same. What I have given to you, give it away for free." (Matthew 10:1-15)

This reminded me of a woman, let's call her Joan, who was preaching on television. Joan gave a word about this back in 2015, "God is rising up the unknown to give away for free what His anointed are charging for."

Directly after hearing Joan's words God kept me awake until 4 A.M. giving me the amazing revelation that led me to write "Why Doesn't God Speak to Me?" He said, "How much are you willing to hear from Me? To receive from Me?"

Instantly, I replied, "You have given me glimpses of the price I may have to pay, and I am now ready and willing. I give it all to you...should the price be my very life."

The quiet voice of the Holy Spirit continued, "Then implement the revelation I gave to you when I revealed why John was taken back in time to old Jerusalem."

"I am, God, aren't I?" I asked. "Ever since You spoke to me about going to Heaven, I am putting your revelations on my website for free.

And I will never charge for a prayer or an appearance."

"But you are charging for your books."

The words caused a mild panic. I couldn't stop my thoughts, "They are my biographies... Everyone charges for a composed biography. And, I paid thousands for a top-of-the-line edit on those, not to mention the cost of having the covers professionally designed. Surely I am able to charge for the final polished project I invested money and years of time creating."

He asked, "What makes these books worth buying? Why do you have a product to sell?"

I knew better than to say, "Because I am able to write in a way that seems to appeal to some people." The word tells us that He knew us before we were formed in the womb; He designed me with the gift to write. Instead I thought, "Because I have had an interesting journey that may help others."

Gently He prodded, "And what did you do to deserve those 'interesting' experiences?"

A part of me wanted to say "I fell in love with Jesus with my whole heart." But I know many people who love Him as I do, and yet they haven't been blessed with some of the wonderful experiences I have been given. My soul sighed as I was forced to admit, "Nothing. I am no one. I abandoned You. And You chose to reveal who You are to me. I messed up time and time again, and You sent miracle after miracle to encourage me... These books wouldn't exist without You." Peace, so strong it was undeniable, welled up deep inside me confirming I was on the right track.

Despite the hours of deep revelation God had just brought to me, petulant, whiny thoughts burst forth, "But all the big evangelists and even smaller pastors have made millions, if not billions, with their books! Why did you have to reveal this to *me*? Why do *I* have to be the one to do it for free?"

"To whom much is given, much is required. You now know the fullness of your calling. You cannot give the enemy a place from which to attack you."

Vividly, the words I uttered less than an hour ago came to my mind: I had said I would do anything He asked. Another soul-sigh, "I put my faith in You to provide. As soon as I can write this up and upload the revised book, they are all yours."

This is why all books associated with "God stuff" are now free in all distribution. The printed copy is free (including shipping) on my website. Occasionally, Amazon begins charging for the ebook without notifying us. We address this issue as soon as we are able so that it will be free around the world. Feel free to read the Kindle version of the book and return it the next day or two for a full refund if you had to pay for it.

Second Word

The next thing God did was to bring me the rest of Bible verses I needed to help correct the situation with His people. God's people who are receiving instructions and help have an instrumental part to play as well. If you continue reading in Matthew, Jesus tells His disciples not to take anything with them, no gold, not even extra clothes:

> ...for the workman deserves his support (his living, his food). (Matthew 10:10)

Giving freely allows the recipient to decide what the revelation is worth to them and to respond, acknowledging that they received something of value from Him. This God's way.

When we give, it is not to the person, it says, "God, I believe You have sent this person and accept that this message is from You." This allows Him to respond to your act of obedience and flow more powerfully into your life.

Here are two more verses in the New Testament on that topic:

> If we have sown [the seed of] spiritual good among you, [is it too] much if we reap from your material benefits?... [On the same principle] the Lord directed that those who publish the good news (the Gospel) should live (get their maintenance) by the Gospel. (Corinthians 9:11&14 AMPC)

> Let him who receives instruction in the Word [of God] share all good things with his teacher [contributing to his support]. Do not be deceived and deluded and misled; God will not allow Himself to be sneered at (scorned, disdained, or mocked by mere pretensions or professions, or by His precepts being set aside.) [He inevitably deludes himself who attempts to delude God.] For whatever a man sows, that and that only is what he will reap. (Galatians 6:6 AMPC)

This is the correct order that God shows us in His word. First, we give what God has revealed to us freely, then we wait for God to speak to those who have received it. You decide what to give: it is a matter between God and the person who has received something of value and it is completely in their hands. What is going on now is backward: we give for a price, collecting before we even know if what we have given has helped others.

Notice the warning at the end of the second verse. If you receive something of spiritual value from God and don't respond according to His way of doing things, you won't benefit from what you are learning. Responding in the way God tells us to not only acknowledges that this has come from Him but it also opens up the door for God to move with power concerning that revelation. Think of it as giving God the "thumbs up" for God to move into your life where this knowledge is concerned.

This was so ingrained in God's people that a group of Christians asked Paul not to come and speak to them because they didn't want to have to give him an offering for his teaching. (2 Corinthians Chapters 11 & 12)

Those who are anointed by God to do His work, who provide spiritually for His people should get there substance from that work. I hope you will pray and ask God what you should give in return *only* if you have received spiritual insight, new information, peace, hope, or encouragement.

God has an amazing sense of humor. I am a publisher who is giving away books for free. It took some time, but I am finally okay with that. I am doing it God's way.

If you have received something of spiritual value, God has instructed me to include three ways in this book in which you can give back to honor Him for what you have received, should you be inclined to do so:

1. Send what God tells you to:

    > Lynn Hardy
    > P.O. Box 234
    > Star, Idaho 83669

2. PayPal – If you have an account, do the following:
    a. Click on "Send Money" then select "to friend or relative"
    b. Type in this email address: LynnHardyCoH@gmail.com
    c. Type in the amount God tells you to give

3. Visit Agape-CF.org and click on "DONATE". It will take you to a page where there are many options to use a credit card to give without or without a PayPal account.

Whatever you decide, may God bless you and keep you.

Free Books by Lynn Hardy

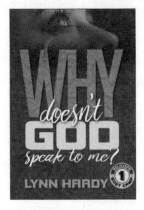

Why Doesn't God Speak to Me?

Believers' Boot Camp
Volume One

Eager hearts cry out, hoping for a single word to confirm that He hears us. Yet, many times the only sound is silence. Over the years I have heard several reasons why God speaks to some and not to others. One night, as I tossed and turned, I brought each of these reasons before the Lord, stating why each of them did not line up with who I thought He was.

Words rose from my soul, pleading for Him to reveal why He has remained silent when a single word from Him would mean so much to so many. For the next few hours, God used things I learned about years ago and things I had just discovered to show why He talks to some and why He doesn't, and in demonstrative ways. In His grace, He also showed me how people could hear more from Him. Thank you for taking time to consider the answers I received and share with you now.

Free on Kindle, Nook & iBooks
Free Printed copies at Agape-CF.org

Destroying Curses in the Courts of Heaven

Believers' Boot Camp
Volume 3

Our rights to appear in the Courts of Heaven have been greatly undervalued. The missing key to our authority is here. Jesus has provided the access and the Bible shows us the court procedures. When we learn to operate in our rightful place as children of the Most High, the enemy will be defeated and we will see the victory we have prayed for.

The death of Jesus freed us from the curse of the Law: we don't go to Hell for our sins. However, they can still give Satan access to us while we are on Earth. We must declare this freedom just as we must make a declaration for our salvation.

➢ Can curses be passed to our children?
➢ What are signs of a curse?
➢ How do you get rid of one?

Every answer is backed by scripture. Come and find out how easy it is to be free!

Roadmap to Heaven

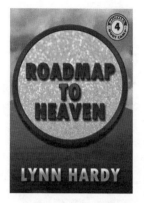

Believers' Boot Camp
Volume 4

As I meditated and sought the Lord, a vision overcame me. A "Roadmap to Heaven" was deposited into my soul. We are entering a season of unparalleled access to Heaven. Jesus is calling all who are His to visit with Him in the Secret Place of the Most High.

➢ What is the Secret Place?
➢ How do we enter?
➢ What will we find there?

The Bible holds the answers, the mystery has been revealed. As you use the map given in this book to journey to the Secret Place, discover your destiny and find the gifts the Holy Spirit will bring along the way.

Order copies at:
Amazon Kindle – Nook – iBooks

Angels Believe in You

Over a thirteen years period Lynn Hardy has...

> Heard the voice of God
> Received two undeniable physical signs from God
> Seen angels and demons on thirteen separate occasions
> Been healed three times from serious and fully documented medical conditions

Have you ever wondered...

❖ What do angels and demons look like?
❖ How can angels help us?
❖ What proof do we have that angels are among us?
❖ What power do we have over demons?

Inside the pages of "Angels Believe in You" you will find some surprising answers.

Make no mistake; Lynn does not claim to be an expert on angels or demons. She is neither the epitome of Christian perfection, nor a Bible scholar. However, what happened to her is both astounding and irrefutable.

It is Lynn's sincere hope that these extraordinary events that have changed her life will comfort and help you through whatever challenges you face — now or in the future.

Notes on Sources

Unfortunately, I am unable to recommend or give any references to any of the religious leaders who are alive today that I have been guided by because of the products they are selling. God has been very clear: to do this would be adding to what they will be judged for. I will only recommend products and people who come up to this higher standard that God has set: All revelation brought by Him must be FREE!

---

[i] "Thayer's Greek-English Lexicon of the New Testament" by Joseph Thayer, New York American Book Co. 1889

[ii] "Foothills Fire" by Joel Jaszewski; *Idaho Statesman*, July 1, 2016